Commendations

From Th

'[**Prof. Stephen Hawking**] is most interested in your impressive proposal.'
● 'In all of written history there are only 2 or 3 people who've been able to think on this scale about the human condition.' **Dr Anthony Barnett**, Prof. of Zoology ● '*FREEDOM* is the book that saves the world…cometh the hour, cometh the man.' **Prof. Harry Prosen**, Pres. Canadian Psychiatric Assn. ● 'I am stunned and honored to have lived to see the coming of "Darwin II"', **Prof. Stuart Hurlbert**, esteemed ecologist ● 'Living without this understanding is like living back in the stone age, that's how massive the change it brings is!' **Prof. Karen Riley**, clinical pharmacist ● 'Frankly, I am blown away by the ground-breaking significance of this work.' **Dr Patricia Glazebrook**, Prof. of Philosophy ● 'I've no doubt a fascinating television series could be made based upon this.' **Sir David Attenborough** ● '*FREEDOM* is the necessary breakthrough in the critical issue of needing to understand ourselves.' **Dr David J. Chivers**, former Pres. Primate Society of Britain ● 'Whack! Wham! I was converted by Griffith's erudite explanation for our behaviour.' **Macushla O'Loan**, *Executive Women's Report* ● 'This is indeed impressive.' **Dr Roger Lewin**, preeminent science writer ● 'I have recommended Griffith's work for his razor-sharp biological clarifications.' **Dr Scott Churchill**, Prof. of Psychology ● 'An original and inspiring understanding of us.' **Dr Charles Birch**, Prof. of Zoology ● 'The insights are fascinating and pertinent and must be disseminated.' **Dr George Schaller**, preeminent biologist ● 'Very impressive, particularly liked the primatology section.' **Dr Stephen Oppenheimer**, geneticist, author *Out of Eden* ● 'I consider the book to be the work of a prophet.' **Dr Ron Strahan**, former dir. Sydney Taronga Zoo ● 'You never forget the moment when you realise this really does explain the human condition.' **Brian Carlton**, broadcaster & media personality ● 'I believe you're on to getting answers to much that has bewildered humans.' **Dr Ian Player**, famous Sth. Afr. conservationist ● 'A superb book, a forward view of a world of humans no longer in naked competition.' **Dr John Morton**, Prof. of Zoology ● 'This might bring about a paradigm shift in the self-image of humanity.' **Dr Mihaly Csikszentmihalyi**, Prof. of Psychology ● 'As a therapist this is a simply brilliant explanation.' **Jayson Firmager**, founder of *Holistic Therapist Magazine* ● 'The questions you raise stagger me into silence; most admirable.' **Ian Frazier**, author *Great Plains* bestseller ● 'The WTM is an island of sanity in a sea of madness.' **Tim Macartney-Snape**, world-leading mountaineer & twice Order of Australia recipient

Commendations From The General Public

'Griffith should be given Nobel prizes for peace, biology, medicine; actually every Nobel prize there is!' ● 'He nailed it, nailed the whole thing, just like the world going from FLAT to ROUND, BOOM the WHOLE WORLD CHANGES, no joke.' ● '*FREEDOM* will be the most influential, world-changing book in history, and time will now be delineated as BG, before Griffith, or AG, after Griffith.' ● 'I'm speechless – this is bigger than natural selection & the theory of relativity!' ● 'I really think this man will become recognized as the best thinker this world's ever seen, and don't we need him right now!' ● 'Griffith has decoded the human species, we FINALLY know what's going on & the suffering stops!' ● 'The world can't deny this for much longer, let the light in, save the human race!' ● 'This is the most exciting moment in my life. *THE Interview* tore my hat off & let my brain fly into the sky!' ● '*THE Interview* should be globally broadcast daily. The healing explanation humans so sorely need.' ● 'In a world that's lost its way there's no greater breakthrough, water to a world dying of thirst.' ● 'Dawn has come at Midnight! A brilliant exposition, we could be on the cusp of regaining Paradise!' ● 'This man has broken the great silence, defeated our denial, got the truth up, woken us from a great trance.' ● 'Beware the 'deaf effect; your mind will initially resist the issue of our corrupted condition and so find it hard to take in or hear what's being said, but if you're patient you'll find the redeeming explanation of our condition pure relief.' ● 'John Lennon pleaded "just give me some truth", well this site finally gives us *all* the truth!' ● '*FREEDOM* is the most profound book since the Bible, now with the redeeming truth about us humans.' ● '*Death by Dogma* is brilliant clarification.' ● 'We were given a computer brain, but no program for it; but Aha, Griffith has found it, made sense of our lives!' ● 'This just goes deeper & deeper in explaining us, like dawn devouring darkness, amazing!' ● 'Agree, this is not another deluded, pseudo idealistic, PC, 'woke', false start to a better world, but the human-condition-resolved real solution.' ● 'Freedom indeed! What we have here is the second coming of innocence who exposes us but sets us free!' ● 'As prophesised, King Arthur has returned to save us (mentioned in par.1036 *Freedom*)' ● 'We all need to go back to school & learn this truthful explanation of life.' ● 'Join in our jubilation, your magic reunites, all men become brothers, all good all bad, be embraced millions! This kiss [of understanding] for the whole world' – From Beethoven's 9th (par.1049 *Freedom*)

The Great Transformation

How understanding the human condition actually transforms the human race

**Jeremy Griffith, Anthony Gowing
& the Akritidis family**

Watch the video of this presentation at
www.HumanCondition.com/transformation

OR

Scan code to view

The Great Transformation: How understanding the human condition actually transforms the human race by Jeremy Griffith, Anthony Gowing & the Akritidis family

Published in 2023, by WTM Publishing and Communications Pty Ltd (ACN 103 136 778) (www.wtmpublishing.com).

 All enquiries to:

WORLD TRANSFORMATION MOVEMENT®
Email: info@worldtransformation.com
Website: www.humancondition.com or www.worldtransformation.com

The World Transformation Movement (WTM) is a global not-for-profit movement represented by WTM charities and centres around the world.

ISBN 978-1-74129-090-5
CIP – Biology, Philosophy, Psychology, Health

Filming and editing by James Press.
Cover design by Jeremy Griffith, James Press, Tess Watson & Brony FitzGerald.

The drawings by Jeremy Griffith, copyright © Fedmex Pty Ltd (ACN 096 099 286) 1991-2023. Computer graphic of exiting cave by Jeremy Griffith, Marcus Rowell and Genevieve Salter, copyright © Fedmex Pty Ltd (ACN 096 099 286) 2009.

Contents

Background

Jeremy Griffith is an Australian biologist who has dedicated his life to bringing redeeming and psychologically healing biological understanding to the dilemma of the human condition—which is the underlying issue in all human life of our species' extraordinary capacity for what has been called 'good' and 'evil'.

Jeremy has published over ten books on the human condition, including:

— *Beyond The Human Condition* (1991), his widely acclaimed second book;

— *A Species In Denial* (2003), an Australasian bestseller;

— *FREEDOM: The End Of The Human Condition* (2016), his definitive treatise;

— *THE Interview* (2020), the transcript of acclaimed British actor and broadcaster Craig Conway's world-changing and world-saving interview with Jeremy about his book *FREEDOM*;

— *Death by Dogma: The biological reason why the Left is leading us to extinction, and the solution* (2021), which presents the biological reason why Critical Theory threatens to destroy the human race;

— *The Great Guilt that causes the Deaf Effect* (2022), which describes how lifting the great burden of guilt from the human race initially causes a 'Deaf Effect' difficulty taking in or 'hearing' what's being presented;

— *The Shock Of Change that understanding the human condition brings* (2022), which addresses how to manage the shock of change that inevitably occurs when the redeeming understanding of our corrupted condition arrives;

— *Therapy For The Human Condition* (2023), which is about the therapy that is desperately needed to rehabilitate the human race from our psychologically upset state or condition, elaborating on what is presented in *FREEDOM*; and

— *Our Meaning* (2023), which explains how being able to know and fulfil the great objective and meaning of human existence finally ends human suffering.

This booklet, **The Great Transformation: How understanding the human condition actually transforms the human race** is a transcript of a presentation Jeremy and others gave in 2023 (which can be viewed at www.humancondition.com/transformation) about how understanding the human condition can save humanity from the imminent threat of extinction from terminal levels of psychosis.

Jeremy's work has attracted the support of such eminent scientists as the former President of the Canadian Psychiatric Association Professor Harry Prosen, the esteemed ecologist Professor Stuart Hurlbert, Australia's Templeton Prize-winning biologist Professor Charles Birch, the Former President of the Primate Society of Great Britain Dr David Chivers, Nobel Prize-winning physicist Stephen Hawking, as well as other distinguished thinkers such as the pre-eminent philosopher Sir Laurens van der Post.

Jeremy is the founder and a patron of the World Transformation Movement (WTM)—see www.HumanCondition.com.

The Great Transformation
How understanding the human condition actually transforms the human race

Jeremy Griffith's presentation

Jeremy Griffith presenting *The Great Transformation*, 2023

[1]Welcome to this June 2023 presentation titled *The Great Transformation: How understanding the human condition actually transforms the human race*. I'm Jeremy Griffith, an Australian biologist, and I'm in a studio at one of our World Transformation Movement (WTM) offices in Sydney, Australia. And before I begin, it might be of assistance to print out this transcript of the talk to help you follow the presentation.

Part 1. Jeremy Griffith describes how finding the redeeming understanding of the human condition was the hard part for the human race, however we still have to apply the understanding to free ourselves from the human condition

[2] The first part of this talk will explain that while finding the redeeming understanding of the human condition was the hard part for the human race, the problem is that we still have to apply the understanding to free ourselves from the human condition.

[3] As I summarise in my introductory video and booklet, *THE Interview That Solves The Human Condition And Saves The World!*, and I fully explain in my definitive book *FREEDOM: The End Of The Human Condition*, humanity's heroic journey of painstakingly accumulating knowledge has finally led to the finding of the redeeming understanding of our psychologically upset, soul-corrupted *human condition*—thus ending all the conflict and suffering in human life at its source, and providing the now urgently needed path forward for the complete rehabilitation and transformation of our lives and world!

[4] SO WHAT I'M GOING TO BE PRESENTING IS THE ACTUAL ROAD MAP THAT EVERY HUMAN, AND THE HUMAN RACE AS A WHOLE, IS NOW ABLE TO FOLLOW FOR OUR SPECIES' PSYCHOLOGICAL REHABILITATION. And I think everyone would agree that psychological rehabilitation is precisely what the human race now urgently needs!

[5] So yes, as I summarised in *THE Interview*, our whole human journey of conscious thought and enquiry has finally led to the discoveries by science of the differences in the way genes and nerves process information—that genes can *orientate* a species but the nerve-based, fully conscious mind that we humans have needs to *understand* the world to operate—with the resulting conflict

between our instincts and intellect *unavoidably* causing our psychologically upset, soul-corrupted human condition. And this ability to know *why* we fully conscious humans were seemingly so stupid as to corrupt our original all-loving instinctive self or soul is the *redeeming* insight we have needed to *relieve* this core insecurity about our corrupted condition that we have carried since we became a fully conscious species some 2 million years ago (as explained in pars 705-707 of *FREEDOM*, 2 million years ago is when our large association-cortexed, thinking brain first appeared in the fossil record of our ancestors). The great 'burden of guilt' we humans have suffered from for destroying the magic world of our soul has at last been lifted—because we have found <u>the key</u> understanding that ends the underlying pain in our brains and allows the human race to become psychologically secure, happy and sane again!

[6] Indeed, when the ancient Greeks had inscribed on their Temple of Apollo at Delphi the words 'Man, know thyself' they were beseeching us to make sense of, and by so doing bring an end to, all the chaos, suffering and seeming madness in human life. Certainly, humanity has made great progress in understanding the universe around us, but the all-important problem of the human condition remained an unsolved mystery, to the extent that one of history's greatest scientists, Sir Isaac Newton, lamented that 'I can calculate the motion of heavenly bodies but not the madness of people'. Well, through the efforts of all the humans who have ever lived, which eventually enabled science to discover how genes and nerves work, that whole jigsaw of confusion and mystery about us humans *has* now been pieced together so that all the hardship, suffering and 'madness' we humans have been enduring for so long *does* finally make sense. Christ said 'the truth will set you free' (John 8:32), and now at last the ultimate 'truth' of the explanation of our fundamental goodness *has* 'set' us 'free', and the human race *is* finally on its way back home to peace, togetherness and happiness. The light of transforming understanding now comes streaming into Plato's dark cave where he said we have had to hide for fear of exposure of our corrupted condition, which has been a horrible existence of blind confusion and devastation (I'll refer to Plato's cave allegory again shortly). Yes, this liberating light of understanding is going to be so incredibly relieving the human race will feel like it is waking up from a nightmare!

Graphic by J. Griffith, M. Rowell and G. Salter © 2009 Fedmex Pty Ltd

[7] So that is the overall effect of finding *the* 'holy grail' of the redeeming, reconciling and rehabilitating understanding of our species' 2-million-year corrupted condition. We *finally* have the means to achieve the rehabilitated 'wholeness for humans' that the psychoanalyst Carl Jung was forever telling us 'depends on the ability to own our own shadow'—because we CAN now 'own' the 'shadow' of our species' corrupted condition, and so the human race IS finally in a position to become 'whole'. The word 'psychosis' literally means 'soul-illness' and 'psychiatry' literally means 'soul-healing', derived as they are from *psyche* meaning 'soul', *osis* meaning 'abnormal state or condition', and *iatreia* meaning 'healing' (see pars 63 & 72 of *FREEDOM*), but we have never been able to 'heal our soul', in effect explain to our original instinctive self or soul that we, our fully conscious thinking self, is good and not bad and by so doing reconcile and heal our split selves—until now. Which is why Professor Harry Prosen,

a former President of the Canadian Psychiatric Association, said about the psychological effect of this understanding that '**I have no doubt this biological instinct vs intellect explanation of the human condition is the holy grail of insight we have sought for the psychological rehabilitation of the human race.**' And the more we digest this relieving understanding of our fundamental goodness, the more healing relief comes to *every* aspect of our psychologically upset human condition.

[8] Yes, we have finally achieved humanity's dreamed-of goal of finding the redeeming understanding of our now immensely psychologically upset, soul-corrupted, 'fallen' *human condition*. To use the lyrics of the song *The Impossible Dream* from the musical *Man of La Mancha* to illustrate this—throughout humanity's '**glorious quest**' to solve the human condition, we have borne '**the unbearable sorrow**' of our corrupted state, and '**run where the brave dare not go**' and '**march**[ed] **into hell for**' the '**heavenly cause**' of achieving the seemingly '**impossible dream**' of '**right**[ing] **the unrightable wrong**' of the condemnation we have been living with for being corrupted, and finally with our '**last ounce of courage**' vanquished that seemingly '**unbeatable foe**' of our ignorant instincts and '**reach**[ed] **the** [seemingly] **unreachable star**' of the redeeming, dignifying, liberating and healing understanding of our corrupted condition!

[9] It truly is an almost-beyond-imagining fabulous achievement for us humans—to have lived through, and overcome, the psychological hell that we have had to endure for some 2 million years means we have to be the bravest, most courageous and heroic species to have ever lived on Earth!

[10] HOWEVER, OUR SPECIES' GREAT STRUGGLE IS NOT YET OVER BECAUSE WE STILL HAVE TO APPLY THE REDEEMING UNDERSTANDING FAST ENOUGH TO SAVE THE HUMAN RACE FROM THE IMMINENT THREAT OF OUR SPECIES' EXTINCTION FROM TERMINAL LEVELS OF PSYCHOLOGICAL UPSET! As I will explain, the way we do this—and this applies both individually

and collectively—is through the Transformed Way of Living. But before I get into that part of the presentation, the first problem that has to be understood and overcome is the 'Deaf Effect', which I'll now explain.

Part 2. The problem of the 'Deaf Effect'

Plato's analogy of the human race having to hide in a dark cave to avoid exposure of the unbearably depressing issue of their corrupted human condition

[11] As I have described in my video/booklet *The Great Guilt*, and in Video/Freedom Essay 11, and in FAQ 1.16, the only way we humans have been able to cope with the unbearably depressing truth of our corrupted condition while we couldn't explain it was to deny its existence. As I mentioned, the great Greek philosopher Plato used the perfect analogy for this situation when he described us humans as having to hide deep underground in a dark cave where no light could get in and expose our corrupted condition. Well, Plato not only described how we have had to hide in a dark cave-like state of denial

of our corrupted condition, he even predicted what would happen when one day someone puts together the redeeming understanding of that corrupted condition that liberates the cave prisoners from having to hide in their dark cave. Yes, way back during the Golden Age of Greece in 360 BC, when writing in his dialogue *The Republic* about the time when someone **'escapes from the cave into the light of day'** and **'sees for the first time the real world and returns to the cave'** to help the cave prisoners **'Escape into the sun-filled setting outside the cave** [which] **symbolizes the transition to the real world'** ('Plato' in *Encarta Encyclopedia,* by Prof. Robert M. Baird; see www.wtmsources.com/101), Plato wrote that when the cave prisoner is **'forcibly dragged up the steep and rocky ascent** [out of the cave] **and not let go till he had been dragged out into the sunlight** [shown the truthful, **real**, redeeming explanation of **our** corrupted, **imperfect human condition**—and he actually used the term **'human condition'**], **the process would be a painful one, to which he** [the cave prisoner] **would much object, and when he emerged into the light his eyes would be so overwhelmed by the brightness of it that he wouldn't be able to see a single one of the things he was now told were real.'** Significantly, Plato then added, **'Certainly not at first. Because he would need to grow accustomed to the light before he could see things in the world outside the cave'** (*The Republic,* c.360 BC; tr. H.D.P. Lee, 1955, 515-516; see www.wtmsources.com/227).

[12] So Plato has said that when we humans are presented with the redeeming explanation of our corrupted condition we would be so attached to living in denial of it that we 'wouldn't be able to see single one of the things...[we are] now told were real'. It makes *absolute* sense that we humans have been living in such deep fear of the issue of our corrupted condition that our **'first'** response to the arrival of its explanation is to not allow our mind to take in or 'hear' what is being talked about. We suffer from a 'mental block', what we in the WTM have come to describe as the 'Deaf Effect'. And I should emphasise what amazing insight Plato had—no wonder Alfred North (A.N.)

Whitehead, himself one of the most highly regarded philosophers of the twentieth century, described the history of philosophy as being merely **'a series of footnotes to Plato'** (*Process and Reality*, 1979, p.39 of 413). Plato truly was a very great denial-free, honest, effective thinker or what humanity has termed a 'prophet'.

Having to **'grow accustomed to the light'**

[13] So, yes, the problem of the Deaf Effect is very, *very* real—so it is **'certainly'** likely that **'at first'** you, the listener or reader, won't be able to, as Plato said, take in or 'hear' a **'single one of the things'** you are **'now'** being **'told'** are **'real'**! I know that saying that will seem like an impossibility—you will think 'if this explanation is rational I'll be able to understand it'—but the problem of the Deaf Effect is actually true (you can read many real-life accounts of the Deaf Effect in *The Great Guilt* and Freedom Essay 11). So everyone needs

to be warned that they will very likely experience this extraordinary problem of the Deaf Effect when listening to the description and explanation of the human condition.

The initial 'Deaf Effect' reaction to analysis of the human condition

[14] THE GREAT DIFFICULTY THEREFORE THAT THIS PROBLEM OF THE DEAF EFFECT CREATES, IS *HOW CAN IT BE OVERCOME*? Having lived in great fear of the issue of our corrupted condition, how can people overcome that fear enough to be able to look at, take in and absorb the explanation of our corrupted human condition, and by so doing discover that the all-redeeming, all-relieving and fear-ending understanding of that corrupted condition has finally been found?

[15] WELL, THE SOLUTION TO THIS PROBLEM OF THE DEAF EFFECT— THE WAY PEOPLE OVERCOME IT—IS THROUGH BEING PREPARED TO RE-READ AND/OR RE-LISTEN TO WHAT IS BEING WRITTEN OR SAID. This process of re-reading and re-listening to what is in fact a straight-forward and clear presentation—of **'grow[ing] accustomed to the light'** as Plato described it—erodes our historic denial and counters the Deaf Effect, allowing the compassionate and immensely relieving insights to become accessible.

Broadcaster Brian Carlton interviewing Jeremy Griffith in 2014

[16]This comment by the renowned Australian journalist and broadcaster Brian Carlton, made during an interview with me in 2014, demonstrates how perseverance overcomes this problem of the Deaf Effect: **'I was already aware of Jeremy's work. In fact, I interviewed Jeremy on my radio show about one of his earlier books, and I remember when I opened the interview to the listeners to call in there was so much interest the interview went for almost two hours and I'm really not exaggerating…I remember when I first read one of your [Jeremy's] books I went through a stage where I couldn't quite get my head around it. I got about half of it and it was a little confusing and a little dense but I didn't give up. I kept reading it and in time your explanations did start to become clear and it made a hell of a lot of sense to me…The process of stripping off the denial is the difficult part, but once you've done that it's relatively simple from there on in I've found. The answers become glaringly obvious…It's an *intellectual* epiphany… I have a more complete understanding of myself, everybody around me, the society at large, the way the planet works. It's a revelation! I don't use that in a religious sense, it's a quantifiably different thing but it has a similar impact**

on you...It's very simple, it's not hard. The end process, the revelation, if you like, is easy and reassuring and calming and self-accepting. Getting there is the difficult bit...When you *get* it, it is an event. You remember the day, you remember the section of the book, you remember when it happened, it stays with you, it's fresh' (the full interview can be viewed at www.humancondition.com/ carlton-video).

Persevering with the information is how to overcome the 'Deaf Effect'
and access understanding of every aspect of human existence

[17] So, the overall solution to the problem of the Deaf Effect—which has been such a big problem it has been stopping this all-relieving and all-solving explanation of the human condition getting out to the whole world—is to patiently wait for a critical mass of people to appear who have managed 'to grow accustomed to the light' enough to overcome the Deaf Effect (either through their own perseverance, or a rare lack of resistance to the subject of our corrupted human condition) and for the relief and excitement of these people to then inspire the rest of humanity to persevere reading and listening to the explanation of the human condition enough so they can *also* overcome the Deaf Effect and discover the immensely relieving and human-race-saving understanding of our corrupted human condition.

Part 3. The problem of the threat of our species' extinction from terminal levels of psychosis

[18] Okay, once the Deaf Effect can begin to be overcome, the problem then is—and like the Deaf Effect this is also a very serious problem—CAN THE HUMAN RACE BENEFIT FROM THE RELIEVING UNDERSTANDING QUICKLY ENOUGH TO AVOID THE FAST APPROACHING THREAT OF THE EXTINCTION OF OUR SPECIES FROM TERMINAL LEVELS OF PSYCHOSIS?

[19] The situation is that while the human race *has* finally managed to achieve the seeming **'impossible dream'** and **'reach**[ed] **the** [seemingly] **unreachable star'** of finding the redeeming understanding of our corrupted condition, it is now so psychologically exhausted there is a very real possibility it won't be able to benefit from that 2-million-year heroically fought-for breakthrough understanding before it is outrun by and dies from terminal psychosis!

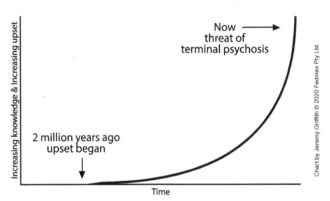

The race between self-destruction and self-understanding

[20] As I explained in *THE Interview*, the history behind this unthinkably horrific situation where the human race is now so psychologically exhausted that it faces the threat of extinction from terminal levels of psychosis—which the above graph summarises—is that we humans have been becoming increasingly psychologically

upset since we first became a fully conscious species and challenged
our instincts for the management of our lives some 2 million years
ago—with extreme upset developing in the last 10,000 years or so
when the development of agriculture made it possible for large
numbers of people to live close together in settlements, which greatly
increased the occurrence and spread of upset—as the historian
Manning Clark said, **'The bush [wilderness] is our source of innocence; the
town is where the devil prowls around'** (see par. 941 of *FREEDOM*). This rapid
increase in upset is what has led to the terminal levels of psychosis
in emerging generations in the world today.

[21] This situation of the psychological exhaustion of younger generations now is in fact very dire—they are so psychologically crippled
and unable to cope with anything that they are being referred to as the
'snowflake' generations. They are even describing *themselves* as **'The
Burnout Generation'** ('How Millennials Became The Burnout Generation', BuzzFeednews.
com, 5 Jan. 2019). In Aspect 1 of my 2023 booklet *Our Meaning*, I present
endless articles reporting on how the psychological exhaustion
everywhere now in the human race, but especially in younger generations, is so great that society is breaking down everywhere we
look and we are entering end game, as it were, for our species!

[22] The following is a compilation of quotes from those articles
(see *Our Meaning* for the sources of the quotes). These reports
speak of an **'epidemic of autism'**, and **'exploding rates'** of **'bipolar disorder'**
and **'ADHD'**, and **'spiralling numbers of children with developmental delay'**,
and **'a tidal wave of mental health issues in the schools'** such as **'anxiety'**,
'depression', **'self-loathing'**, **'fragility'**, **'sadness'**, **'hopelessness'**, **'suicide'**
and **'self-harm'**.

[23] These reports from across the world also tell of how many of
the younger generations are now finding it almost impossible to face
the world, let alone work to earn a living and support humanity's
heroic search for knowledge, ultimately for self-understanding. For
instance, in Australia it is reported that there is **'a silent legion of kids
across our nation'** suffering from this psychological paralysis, where,
'As the organisation School Refusal Australia explained in a submission to

Victoria's royal commission into mental health, "The kids are isolated, often live in their bedrooms 24/7 and are unable to leave their home. They barely function. They feel guilty and ashamed. They've given up"...This is not simply wagging [skipping school], as earlier generations knew it. It's an extreme phobia'. And further reports about the psychological paralysis of the young in Australia state that 'One in five teens struggles to read', and that the paralysis is so great 'we've now got a population that doesn't want to work' and that 'there are thousands of businesses...that just can't get staff, let alone good employees'. The current chair of Australia's national broadcaster, Ita Buttrose, complained that 'Millennials so lack resilience they need hugging'. In China, it is reported that many of the young are now only able to 'do the minimum' and feel 'they cannot find a way out' of their predicament of not wanting to participate in the world. In France, a study claims 'the country is now mired in a "laziness epidemic"'... This unwillingness to work at all has led to a huge shortage of labour'. In Japan, there is now an epidemic of 'shut-ins', 'the phenomenon of withdrawal from society'. A report about Spain said that many 'young Spaniards have dropped out of education and work altogether, with no plans to resume studying or look for a job'. And in the United States, it is reported that among 'Millennials' there is an 'epidemic' of 'narcissism', a 'personality disorder' where 'people try to boost [low] self-esteem', and that their 'self-centredness could bring about the end of civilization'. A survey in the US also found that 'a staggering 79 per cent' of business owners and managers 'find Gen Z the most difficult generation to have in the workplace' citing 'entitlement, a lack of effort, motivation and productivity', some saying that interacting with them 'can be exhausting because they lack discipline' and 'are too easily offended'. So yes, 'The Burnout Generation[s]' is absolutely the right description for what is happening in the human race. [This end-play state of terminal psychosis was actually predicted in the Bible, see 2 Timothy 3:1-5.]

^{24}In the case of politics, I need to firstly explain the basic situation that is involved in the political dialectic, which is that having had to deny the unbearably depressing truth of our 2-million-year corrupted condition while we couldn't explain it, has meant that there has been no corrupted condition to have to be explained, so there's been no admission of our fundamental task and responsibility of having to participate in humanity's heroic battle to find the redeeming explanation of our corrupted condition! <u>If there's no corrupted condition, then there is no corrupted condition to have to be explained!</u> However, now that we *can* explain and defend our corrupted condition, we *can* finally admit the existence of it and therefore of humanity's great, heroic meaning and purpose of having to find understanding of it—which, as I explain in my booklet *Death by Dogma*, is a battle that the right-wing in politics has supported with its emphasis on the freedom of expression and on the upsetting competitive, selfish and aggressive individualism needed to find that ultimate explanation. <u>Admit our corrupted condition and we finally have the reason for the right-wing in politics!</u> John Kenneth Galbraith, the liberal economist and adviser to the Kennedys, once mockingly said that the Right are engaged in **'one of man's oldest, best financed, most applauded, and, on the whole, least successful exercises in moral philosophy. That is, the search for a truly superior moral justification for selfishness'** ('Wealth and Poverty' speech, National Policy Committee on Pockets of Poverty, 13 Dec. 1963). Well, with the explanation for, and resulting ability to admit, our corrupted condition, that **'truly superior moral justification for selfishness'** that the Right have supported is now revealed, along with the extreme danger of the Left's freedom-of-expression-and-selfishness-denying dogmatic, deluded, pseudo idealistic demands for a cooperative, selfless and loving world!

[25] So while there was no corrupted condition to have to be explained and thus no ability to effectively explain and justify the selfishness and competitiveness of the right-wing, the attraction of the Left's incredibly dangerous *pseudo* idealistic, 'let's-all-just-hug-each-other', 'do-good-to-make-yourself-look-and-feel-good', politically correct, 'woke' culture has become irresistible—especially for those who are extremely psychologically exhausted from the effects of humanity's heroic battle to find understanding, namely today's younger generations. After the 2022 federal election

in Australia, 'the Australian National University 2022 Australian Election Study' found that 'only one in four voters under the age of 40 voted for the [right-wing] Coalition and only one in five voters among Generation Z voted for the Coalition'. In fact, there are many predictions being made in democratic countries that before long the right-wing may never be able to win power again [a situation actually predicted in the Bible, see pars 1123-1126 of *FREEDOM*]. A May 2019 article in *The Atlantic* that has the meta title 'Young Democrats May Control the Political Future' says that 'the [right-wing] GOP seems to be playing a losing hand', that it seemingly won't ever get back into power! The take-over by pseudo idealism and with it the destruction of humanity is, apparently, upon us! Thank goodness then that what has actually been right about the right-wing and actually wrong about the left-wing has finally been revealed! Better still, thank goodness the understanding that makes this exposure possible brings to an end the whole upsetting battle to find this all-exposing and all-relieving understanding [and thus an end to politics]!

²⁶ Yes, as I emphasised at the end of *THE Interview*, and in *Death by Dogma*, the *real* way to bring about a cooperative, selfless and loving world was to end the upsetting struggle to find the redeeming understanding of our corrupted human condition, because, as I will talk more about shortly in Part 4 of this presentation, that redeeming understanding is what ends the need for the individualistic competitive, selfish and aggressive world the human race has had no choice but to carry on living in. Finding understanding of the human condition was the real and only way to end our upsetting search for that understanding and save the human race from extinction!

²⁷ I should mention that while my booklet *Death by Dogma* focuses on the extreme danger of the pseudo idealism of the Left, my booklet *Our Meaning* focuses on how being able to admit our corrupted condition finally allows us to admit our species' great meaning and purpose of having to find the redeeming explanation of that corrupted condition, and how being able to now know our meaning brings immense relief to so many aspects of our lives.

[28] To continue on with quotes from those articles about the extent of our psychologically exhausted condition: in the case of education, there are reports that **'half of undergraduate students** [now] **think it is acceptable to silence speech they feel is upsetting'**, but how can you learn and seek truth and meaning, which has been the whole purpose of education, if you aren't prepared, expected or even challenged to think anymore. As one report said, the **'safe-space, trigger warning culture'**, with its **'intolerance of dissent in Western universities and the puritanical hectoring of social media give grounds for concern that the flowering of freedom** [of thought] **in the past several centuries may come under threat… [it] may mean that the entire world is heading into a great endarkenment'**. So yes, humans are giving up on thinking, which is the basic responsibility of being a conscious being! Truly, the breakdown of human civilisation is happening *everywhere*!

[29] And to look at what is happening in our communities, this is a drawing I have done and included in *Death by Dogma* to illustrate the end play, desperately sad dystopia of lawlessness, unbearable psychosis, drug addiction and homelessness that is now tragically a characteristic of the streets of large cities in the US—and what is happening there is where the rest of civilisation is rapidly heading. So there really isn't any meaning or hope left out there in Plato's human-condition-denying cave world—which is why my booklet *Our Meaning* that reveals the meaning of all our suffering is especially needed and precious.

THE DEATH OF HUMANITY

Drawing by J. Griffith © 2021 Fedmex Pty Ltd

[30] The photographs on the left and right below are of people participating in '**post-apocalyptic zombie street parades**' that have become popular among the young in recent times. The painting in the middle by Jean-Michel Basquiat was sold at auction in 2013 for a whopping $US48.8 million, a price no doubt achieved in part because of how much it resonates as an image of our time. While we have had to live in denial of our corrupted condition while we couldn't explain it, that condition has become so extreme that it has become necessary to gain at least *some* psychological relief from it by temporarily giving it expression—exorcism through being honest about it at least for a little while!

Depictions of the terminally alienated, zombie state that humanity has arrived at

[31] These lyrics from the young American heavy metal band 'With Life In Mind' reveal just how traumatising our now immensely upset, soul-corrupted world is for young minds, and therefore how important it is going to be for them to now be able to make sense of that world through understanding the human condition: '**It scares me to death to think of what I have become…I feel so lost in this world**', '**Our innocence is lost**', '**I scream to the sky but my words get lost along the way. I can't express all the hate that's led me here and all the filth that swallows us whole. I don't want to be part of all this insanity. Famine and death. Pestilence and war. A world shrouded in darkness…Fear is driven into our minds everywhere we look**', '**Trying so hard for a life with such little purpose…Lost in oblivion**',

'Everything you've been told has been a [human-condition-avoiding] lie...
We've all been asleep since the beginning of time. Why are we so scared to
use our minds?', 'Keep pretending; soon enough things will crumble to the
ground...If they could only see the truth they would coil in disgust', '<u>How do
we save ourselves from this misery...So desperate for the answers...We're
straining on the last bit of hope we have left. No one hears our cries. And no
one sees us screaming</u>', 'This is the end' (*Grievances* album, 2010).

[32] A 2017 report by medical doctors published by the US's National
Library of Medicine, titled 'We are the hollow men: The worldwide epidemic of mental illness', <u>summarises this whole horror, psychologically
exhausted situation the human race has arrived at</u>. The report begins
by quoting from T.S. Eliot's poem *The Hollow Men*: 'Remember us
– if at all – not as lost / violent souls, but only / as the hollow men / the stuffed
men / This is the way the world ends / not with a bang but a whimper'; and
the report then says, 'All across the world, patients are coming to their
local Accident and Emergency Departments/Casualty Centers (EDs). They
are in pain. <u>Sometimes, their eyes scream out their suffering and other times
they appear as cold, empty shells reflecting the hollowness the patient feels
inside</u>. Unlike patients with compound fractures or lacerations, patients with
psychiatric illness have wounds that are rarely visible to the naked eye. <u>This
is the way the world ends, not with a bang but a whimper</u>. This is the face of
mental illness, the stark picture seen by emergency physicians and psychi-
atrists, with problems ranging from depression to suicide and psychosis, as
well as addictive disorders...The statistics are frightening' and the system
is 'stretched to the breaking point...with no end in sight'.

[33] Yes, it certainly does appear that there is 'no end in sight' to the
descent into terminal psychosis out there; that 'this is the end'!

[34] So, while we have had to live in denial of our psychologically
upset, soul-corrupted, 'fallen' human condition while we couldn't
explain it, now that we can explain and understand it we can—and

now must—FACE THE TRUTH THAT PSYCHOLOGICAL UPSET HAS REACHED EXCRUCIATING, PARALYSING, TERMINAL LEVELS.

[35] And what the truth of this psychologically tortured, truly horrifying predicament means is that even *if* there were innumerable counsellors highly trained and skilled in using the redeeming and healing understanding of the human condition that we now have, and even *if* every person was in therapy all day long, it would still take a number of generations for all the psychological upset in humans to be healed and psychological upset in humans be eliminated from Earth—and for every child to be able to grow up in a completely unconditionally loving environment and so not suffer from any psychological upset during their upbringing.

[36] To illustrate the point, it is obviously going to take a number of generations for the healing effects of the understanding we now have of the human condition for men to not be to some degree egocentric; and for women to no longer need the reinforcement of being sexually attractive—indeed, it will take a number of generations for sex as humans have been practising it under the duress of the human condition to no longer occur! In chapter 8:11B of *FREEDOM* I explain the relationship that has existed between men and women under the duress of the human condition, and also how, while under that duress, sex has been used as a way of violating or destroying or ruining or 'fucking' innocence for its implied criticism of our lack of innocence.

[37] So the reality is that it will take a number of generations to psychologically rehabilitate the human race, which brings us back to the problem of how is the human race supposed to cope with its extreme psychological upset in the meantime? HOW CAN THE CATASTROPHE OF THE IMMINENT DEATH OF OUR SPECIES FROM TERMINAL PSYCHOSIS BE AVOIDED?

Part 4. The Transformed Way of Living

[38] THE ANSWER TO THIS PROBLEM OF HOW WE AVOID EXTINCTION FROM TERMINAL PSYCHOSIS IS THE TRANSFORMED WAY OF LIVING, WHICH I WILL NOW EXPLAIN.

[39] While our species' psychological rehabilitation will take a number of generations, what is so spectacularly wonderful is that having the redeeming understanding of our fundamental goodness immediately obsoletes our old artificial ways of defending ourselves against the implication that our corrupted condition meant we are bad and unworthy. Remember in Part 1 of *THE Interview* that I explained using the Adam Stork analogy how when we were unjustly criticised by our instincts for defying them and managing our life from a basis of understanding, that the only ways we could defend ourselves against our instincts' criticism was to prove that we weren't bad by competitively winning as much power, fame, fortune and glory as we could, and by angrily attacking the implication that we were bad, and by blocking out from our minds that implied condemnation. Well, now that we have found the *real* defence for our corrupted condition of the actual understanding of why we are good and not bad, those old *artificial* egocentric, angry and alienated ways of defending ourselves are necessarily obsoleted. Those old defences have done their job and are no longer needed.

[40] Indeed, now that we have the *real* defence for our corrupted condition of the 'instinct vs intellect' biological explanation for why we corrupted ourselves, and therefore why we are actually good and not bad, it would be completely irresponsible given the plight of the world to continue using the now obsoleted, and thus now unnecessarily destructive, old *artificial* angry, egocentric and alienated ways of defending ourselves! With the real defence for our corrupted condition found, everyone can, and now must if we are to save the human race, abandon our old artificial ways of maintaining their sense of self-worth, and instead direct all our abilities and energies to supporting the redeeming understanding

of the human condition that we now have and to adopting the co-operative, selfless and loving new way of living that it has made possible; indeed, that it has revealed we have no reason not to take up. We let go of our old, now obsoleted, selfish preoccupation with winning power, fame, fortune and glory as the way to sustain our sense of self-worth, and instead focus our mind on living for and through the fabulous cooperative, selfless and loving new potential that has opened up for the human race now that understanding of our corrupted human condition has been found and our soul/instinct and intellect are reconciled. Everyone now can and has to change from—be transformed from—being servants of our egos to being servants of humanity. We *had to* defensively defy our instincts to find understanding, ultimately self-understanding, understanding of why we corrupted our instinctive soul, so our egocentric defensive system was necessary, but now it no longer is.

The reconciling understanding between our instinct and intellect that ends the need
for our artificial angry, egocentric and alienated ways of defending ourselves

[41] And, gloriously, what happens when we give up our old angry, egocentric and alienated way of living and take up this new Transformed Way of Living where we live in support of the understanding of the human condition is we discover a freedom we have only ever dreamed of where we are no longer preoccupied

justifying ourselves and proving our worth every minute of the day, as we actually *have* been every minute of the day, and as a result are finally able to access all the true beauty of our lives, of those around us, and of every living thing. The shackles of the responsibility we have had of having to continue supporting and participating in humanity's immensely necessary and immensely heroic but at the same time immensely upsetting, soul-corrupting search for the redeeming understanding of why we defied our instincts fall away and a whole new world that is effectively free of the agony of the human condition opens up for us. Even though we are not yet free of the psychologically upset state of our personal corrupted condition, we are *effectively* free of it, our lives are effectively transformed, because it is no longer the focus of our minds. That is the seemingly magic immediate benefit of having the redeeming biological understanding of the human condition: we all—Baby Boomers, X-gen'ers, Y/Millennials, Z-gen'ers and Alpha-gen'ers—are suddenly free to live our lives in support of a non-competitive, non-selfish, non-aggressive and non-human-corrupted-condition-denying, peaceful and truthful, human-race-saving, cooperative, selfless and loving way of living that is effectively free of the agony of the human condition. SO THIS IS HOW WE ARE QUICKLY ABLE TO BRING THE HUMAN RACE BACK FROM THE BRINK OF EXTINCTION FROM TERMINAL LEVELS OF PSYCHOSIS.

The human-race-saving and all-exciting Transformed Way of Living

[42] Now, it should be very clear from the brief explanation of politics given in Part 3 above, that <u>this is *not* the horrifically deluded, human-race-destroying false start to a transformed loving world that the politically correct, 'woke' movement is dogmatically trying to impose</u>, but the human condition redeemed and reconciled UNDERSTANDING-BASED *real* transformation of the human race—however, this distinction is so important it needs to be emphasised. In my book *Death by Dogma*—especially in paragraphs 85-86—I describe just how dishonest and extremely dangerous is the **'fake it to make it'** false start to a transformed world that the PC 'woke' movement is dogmatically trying to impose.

[43] <u>I should also emphasise that while this great transformation of the human race that understanding of the human condition makes possible is similar to a religious transformation in that it involves completely letting go of, or transcending, or being 'born again' from, our real, upset self and instead deferring to another way of living, that is where the similarity ends.</u> As I explain in chapter 9:5 of *FREEDOM*, while religions were an incredibly effective means of containing the upset in humans while the search for understanding of that upset condition was being carried out, the Transformed Way of Living is, in complete contrast, concerned with what happens *after* that liberating understanding is found and there's no longer any need for the old, must-prove-our-worth, competitive, selfish and aggressive way of living. <u>While religions were human-condition-*relieving*, they were not human-condition-*resolving* like the understanding we are now able to live in support of is.</u>

[44] In fact, the Transformed Way of Living, or <u>Transformed Lifeforce State (TLS)</u> as we in the WTM also refer to it, <u>represents the *realisation* of religion's hope and faith that the liberating *understanding* of the human condition would one day be found</u>—the time <u>Moses</u> looked forward to when he anticipated that we will **'be like God, knowing'** (Bible, Gen. 3:5), with 'God' being humanity's personification of Integrative Meaning (see chapter 4 of *FREEDOM*, or Freedom Essay 23). And it is the time <u>Christ</u> instructed us to pray for in his *Lord's Prayer*

when 'Your [Godly, integrated, peaceful] **kingdom come, your will** [that we be integrative] **be done on earth as it is in heaven'** (Bible, Matt. 6:10 & Luke 11:2). And it is the time predicted in Revelations in the Bible when '**Another book** [will be]...**opened which is the book of life** [the human-condition-explaining and humanity-liberating book]...[and] **a new heaven and a new earth** [will appear] **for the first heaven and the first earth** [will have]...**passed away**...[and the dignifying full truth about our corrupted condition] **will wipe every tear from**...[our] **eyes. There will be no more death or mourning or crying or pain** [i.e. no more insecurity, suffering or sickness], **for the old order of things has passed away'** (20:12, 21:1, 4). And it is the time the great Hebrew prophet Isaiah hoped for when he said humans '**will beat their swords into plough-shares...Nation**[s] **will...**[not] **train for war any more'** (Isa. 2:4). And it is the time when Buddha said that '**In the future they will every one be Buddhas** [be free of psychosis] / **And will reach Perfect Enlightenment** [in other words, reach understanding of the human condition]' (*The Lotus Sutra*, c.560-480 BC, ch.9; tr. W.E. Soothill, 1987, p.148 of 275).

[45] Yes, unlike religion, the Transformed Way of Living represents the *end* of dogma, faith and belief and the beginning of knowing. Essentially, religions were based on deferring to, and living through support of the *embodiment of the ideals* in the form of the soundness and truth of the denial-free-thinking-and-behaving prophet around whom the religion was founded, whereas the Transformed Way of Living is based on deferring to and living through support of first-principle-based biological *understandings of the ideals and of our species' unavoidable historical lack of compliance with those ideals*.

[46] Another immense difference between the Transformed State and a religion is that in the Transformed State there is no deity involved, or deference to a personality; in fact, there is no worship of any kind. And best of all, unlike religion, there is no involvement

or emphasis on guilt, because guilt—and the whole notion of 'good and evil'—has been eliminated forever with the reconciling understanding of the human condition.

[47] As I explain in detail in chapter 9 of *FREEDOM*, the logic behind making this human-race-saving decision to transform our lives by living in support of an anger-egocentricity-and-alienation-obsoleted, understanding-based, cooperative, selfless and loving existence is irrefutable. Now that the great goal of the whole human journey of conscious thought and enquiry is achieved and we have found the redeeming understanding of our corrupted condition, all our old retaliatory, defensive and insecure behaviours of egocentricity, anger and alienation that we had to employ to psychologically prop ourselves up while we couldn't defend ourselves with understanding, are no longer needed. In fact, as I pointed out above, with this redeeming understanding of the human condition found, it would be an act of *total irresponsibility, indeed madness*, to continue down that old, insecure, defensive and now destructive road. The truth is there is nothing in the way now of every human taking up a magnificent, unburdened, human-condition-free, *transformed* life—and as a result, the human race *will* bounce back from the edge of the dark abyss of the threat of extinction to the sun-drenched uplands of a whole new, immensely exciting and immensely relieving potential!

[48] Yes, this totally responsible—and desperately needed—transformation of the human race where everyone lives in support of a cooperative, selfless and loving existence is the way the human race is able to quickly turn around the dire situation it is in and avoid imminent self-destruction from terminal levels of psychosis. We are rational creatures, and so when all the logic says there is only one response we can make, namely the Transformed Way of Living, then that is the only course the human race can, will and must take. The reason we developed science—which is a word that is actually derived from the Latin *scientia*, which means 'knowledge'—is because we are self-adjusting, knowledge-seeking, thinking beings who depend on understanding to manage our lives. And most importantly and relievingly, what this knowledge-based, self-adjusting capability means is that this great transformation of the human race is not a way of living that has to be dogmatically imposed—there is no authoritarian dictatorship involved. And nor is there any need for any form of forceful social insurrection to take place. All that is required is to spread this logical, fully understandable, science-based, biologically-fully-accountable-and-true, incontestable, absolutely justified and needed, breakthrough understanding of the human condition and it will do all the changing on its own—it is a completely peaceful revolution. WE LIVE IN SUPPORT OF THIS UNDERSTANDING AND IT WILL LOOK AFTER EACH OF US AND THE WORLD—THAT IS THE MANTRA OF THE NEW WORLD FOR THE HUMAN RACE!

[49] Yes, it is the *logic* that now says that everyone can and therefore must leave the obsoleted, wretched-with-horrible-suffering-and-dreadful-conflict, agonisingly psychologically upset angry, egocentric and alienated state, to one where we all live in peace, togetherness and happiness. And so exciting and body-draining-with-relief is this life where we are effectively free from the agony of the

human condition that before long, when news of this holy grail of breakthroughs and its ability to transform the human race gets out into the world, there will be a stampede of people who have joined the human-condition-resolved sunshine multitude on the sunshine highway to the world in sunshine! As the great denial-free thinking prophet, scientist and philosopher Teilhard de Chardin wrote, **'The Truth has to only appear once...for it to be impossible for anything ever to prevent it from spreading universally and setting everything ablaze'** (*Let Me Explain*, 1966; tr. René Hague et al., 1970, p.159 of 189).

[50] As I summarise in paragraph 1166 of *FREEDOM*, the excitement and relief of being effectively free of the human condition—the joy and happiness of being liberated from the burden of our insecurities, self-preoccupations and devious strategising; the awesome meaning and power of finally being *genuinely* aligned with the truth and *actually* participating in the magic true world; the wonderful empathy and equality of goodness and fellowship that understanding of the human condition now allows us to feel for our fellow humans; the freedom now to effectively focus on repairing the world; and, above all, the radiant aliveness from the optimism that comes with knowing our species' march through hell has finally ended and that a human-condition-free new world is coming—CAN NOW TRANSFORM EVERY HUMAN AND THUS THE WORLD; hence we are the World Transformation Movement, WTM!

[51] As I have said in every main publication I have ever written, going right back to my first book *Free* in 1988, **'soon from one end of the horizon to the other will appear an army in its millions to do battle with human suffering and its weapon will be understanding'**.

[52] So, the Transformed Way of Living is the way the human race is able to change quickly enough to avoid the imminent threat of self-destruction from terminal levels of psychosis.

Part 5. Sir James Darling's astonishing vision fulfilled

Sir James Ralph Darling (1899-1995)

[53] My headmaster when I was a student at Geelong Grammar School (GGS) in Victoria, Sir James Darling, actually focused on the crucial need for this fundamental change from living selfishly to living selflessly in one of his many extraordinary speeches. Before referring to that speech, I should point out that Sir James was described in his 1995 full-page obituary in *The Australian* newspaper as **'a prophet in the true biblical sense'** (3 Nov. 1995; see www.wtmsources.com/165), and widely recognised as Australia's greatest ever educator; indeed, he was knighted 'for services to education and broadcasting'. Also,

he created at GGS a school of such renown that King Charles III was sent halfway around the world to attend it for part of his education.

King Charles III (on the right) at GGS's Timbertop campus in 1966, which he has described as **'by far the best part'** of his education

[54] So this is what Sir James said in his amazing 1950 GGS Speech Day address: **'selfishness is, as it has ever been, the ultimately destructive force in a society, and there are only two cures for selfishness — the regimented state which we all profess to dislike, and the <u>change of heart</u>, which we refuse to make. <u>That is the choice, believe me, for each one of us, and we have not much time in which to make it. The need for decision</u>** [to have a **'change of heart'** and live selflessly] **<u>is serious and urgent, and the sands</u>** [of time] **<u>are running out</u>'** (Weston Bate, *Light Blue Down Under*, 1990, p.219 of 386). Yes, as my explanation of the human condition finally makes understandable, selfishness has been necessary during humanity's heroic search for understanding of its corrupted condition, however it is still, as Sir James said, **'<u>the ultimately</u> destructive force in a society'**. And yes, the pseudo idealistic dogma of the left-wing in politics' **'regimented state'** is **'dislik**[able]**'**. And yes, as we can now understand, we have had to **'refuse to make' 'the change of heart'** to living selflessly while we still

had to persevere with our corrupting search for understanding of our divisive, corrupted, 'fallen' human condition, *but now that we have found that understanding* we can have that '**cure for selfishness**' of '**the change of heart**' to living selflessly that Sir James emphasised even 73 years ago now back in 1950 was '**serious and urgent**' because '**the sands** [of time] **are running out**'.

[55] Absolutely astonishing as it is, Sir James's vision at GGS was actually to preserve the innocent souls of the boys attending his school in the hope that one of them might remain sound enough to achieve humanity's seemingly '**impossible dream**' of finding the redeeming understanding of our corrupted human condition that makes Sir James's '**change of heart**' to living selflessly possible—which is what I have done, in large measure due to his unique Platonic, soul-preserving-rather-than-intellect-emphasising approach to education. You can read an essay I have written about Sir James's absolutely astonishing, world-saving, Plato-inspired vision of producing a man who would solve the human condition at www. humancondition.com/darling, but the following are some extracts from his various speeches that reveal his outrageously optimistic, clear-sighted and courageous vision—honestly, what I am going to read out must be amongst the most impressive words ever spoken in human history. [The dashes indicate a change from one speech to another, and you can find the sources of the quotes in that essay]: '**Only in the light of…a discovered purpose can we lead Australia into an attitude of mind which is prepared for sacrifice and service…in seeking for such purpose it will be necessary to seek below the surface…**[for the] **thoughts which do lie too deep for tears** [which are those thoughts that for most people are so depressing and confronting they can't go near them, namely thoughts about our corrupted human condition]…**Only so can we come to a better understanding of life, to answer even the all-important question: "What is man that thou art mindful of him** [why is human behaviour so often less than ideal], **and the son of man that thou visitest him?"** [when Christ's behaviour by contrast was sound and ideal—Sir James has here clearly stated that the '**all-important question**' that we have '**to answer**' is the issue of our species'

less-than-ideal, soul-corrupted, 'fallen' human condition.] **For to exclude that question from the study of evolution...**[is] **surely as futile as to talk theology and to forget evolution** [a biologist is going to be needed]**? There must be a complete answer; there must be coherence and sense in the universe; and, until we find it, our thinking is degenerated into disintegration, and our existence fragmented into a rubbish-heap of shreds and patches, with coherence, significance, and growth impossible, our compass-bearings lost, and civilization foundering...Canon Raven, says, the future lies not with the predatory** [selfish] **and the immune** [alienated] **but with the sensitive** [innocent/sound] **who live dangerously** [defy the fragile, insecure world of denial]. **It should be the prime object of education...to develop this sensitivity...the truly sensitive mind is both susceptible and penetrating: it is open to new ideas, and it seeks truth at the bottom of the well. It is the development of this sort of mind which it should be the object of the educational process to cultivate'** — **'each of us should regard our lives as pledged to the one paramount purpose of saving the world...the sands of time are running out'** — While referring to **'the kind of man needed to save Australia and humanity'**, Sir James spoke about cultivating **'men of conscience...men not afraid of facing unpleasant** [truthful] **facts'** — **'It requires more toughness to resist the world** [of denial] **than to join in...It is the awakening and vivifying of the conscience** [innocent soul] **of those who belong to it which ought to be the chief purpose of a Church school... because...conscience is the executive part of consciousness'** — **'The quality which, above all other, needs to be cultivated** [in education] **is sensitivity...on one proviso: he must be sensitive *and* tough** [to solve the human condition and **'save humanity'** requires sufficient sensitivity/innocence/soul to access the truth but also sufficient toughness to stand up to, defy, and ultimately overthrow the all-pervading false and deluded world of denial]. **He must combine tenderness and awareness with fortitude, perseverance, and courage. The sensitivity is necessary because without it there is no life of the mind, no growing consciousness, no living conscience...Can such men be? Of course they can: and they are the leaders whom others will follow. In the world of books there are, for me, Antoine de Saint-Exupéry, or Laurens van der Post** [Sir Laurens is the most quoted author in all my writings, and, incidentally, was who King Charles III chose to be godfather for his eldest son, Prince

William]' — '**The time is past for help which is only a Band-Aid. It is time for radical thinking and for a solution on the grand scale**' — '**We are not now that strength which in old days moved Heaven and Earth...but something ere the end, some work of noble note may yet be done.**'

[56] Yes, how truly astonishing and wonderful was Sir James's bold vision and clarity of thought! Like Plato, Sir James truly was a very great denial-free, honest, effective thinker or prophet, as his obituary recognised.

[57] I should mention that Sir James's focus on cultivating the souls of boys to create '**the kind of man needed to save...humanity**', and the reason why GGS remained a boys-only school during Sir James's tenure, is because — as what he has said above evidences — he knew that it was men's responsibility to solve the human condition. (I provide the biological explanation for why it was men's responsibility in paragraph 770 of *FREEDOM*; in fact that whole chapter 8:11B about the relationship between men and women is relevant description of men's role in the world.) Recklessly unappreciative of Sir James's great vision, GGS became co-educational immediately after Sir James's tenure. So Sir James's extraordinarily bold and truthful world only just lasted long enough to '**cultivate**' the '**sensitivity**' in a '**man**' needed for the '**work of noble note**' to '**be done**' of the '**radical thinking**' '**for a solution on the grand scale**', namely to '**seek truth at the bottom of the well**' and '**answer**' '**the all-important question**' of why '**man**', unlike the '**son of man**', is corrupted, which is the issue of the human condition, before the dishonest, pseudo idealistic, 'do good to make yourself feel and look good', politically correct, 'woke' culture killed his vision! As it says in the Bible, '**was there ever a prophet your fathers did not persecute**' (Acts 7:52) for their truthful clarity.

[58] If boys at GGS didn't have a critically important and enormously difficult job to be prepared for, then co-education would have been ideal, but while that focus existed it *was* pseudo or false idealism to make it co-educational. That is just the truth. As I point out in paragraphs 770-773 of *FREEDOM*, human society hasn't been patriarchal for no reason, and far from males being 'toxic' and society

being 'pale, male and stale', as 'woke' advocates of co-education have said, <u>men have had to be, and now with the human condition solved they have proven to be, the heroes of the story of life on Earth</u>! As one of Australia's most distinguished journalists, Janet Albrechtsen, wrote, and titled her article that defended Sydney's prestigious Cranbrook School remaining a boys-only school, **'The only thing toxic about boys' schools is the woke parents'** (*The Weekend Australian*, 26 Nov. 2022; see www.wtmsources.com/301).

THE AUSTRALIAN ✦

The only thing toxic about boys' schools is woke parents

Behind the scenes of the Cranbrook School drama is
a lesson in how axing single-sex education for boys
promotes bad politics and inequality.

By JANET ALBRECHTSEN

From **Inquirer** November 26, 2022

The Cranbrook School council saga is the quintessential Sydney eastern suburbs story. Billionaires, corporate titans, directors, and investment bankers aplenty

[59] Significantly, <u>my brother Simon</u>, who has been my life-long supporter and basically started the WTM, and <u>my fellow Patron of the WTM and great friend, Tim Macartney-Snape</u>, the world-leading mountaineer who is a twice-honoured Order of Australia recipient, both attended GGS, as did my and Simon's father and Tim's father. Significantly also, Tim's great-great grandfather, Dean Macartney, was one of the founding fathers of GGS. Essentially, it is now up to the WTM to carry on Sir James's vision of **'saving the world'**, which, for the education of young people, we will do by creating schools that teach the redeeming, reconciling and rehabilitating understanding of the human condition, and, since men have completed their job of **'answer**[ing]**...the all-important question'** of why **'man'**, unlike the **'son of man'**, is corrupted, which is the issue of the human condition, these schools will all be co-educational.

Jeremy with his brother Simon (on right), 2018

Jeremy with Tim Macartney-Snape and partner Stacy Rodger, 2023

[60] Yes, the understanding of the human condition and the Transformed Way of Living it brings about achieves Sir James's great **'change of heart'** from living selfishly to living selflessly that is needed to **'save the world'**!

Part 6. Therapising our psychosis

[61] What now needs to be explained is what will complement and help that transformation, and in the long term remove all the psychosis in the human race so there is no longer any need to transcend it with the Transformed Way of Living, IS THE ACTUAL THERAPISING OF OUR PSYCHOSIS THAT THE REDEEMING UNDERSTANDING OF OUR CORRUPTED CONDITION NOW MAKES POSSIBLE—which the transition between these two images by William Blake illustrate.

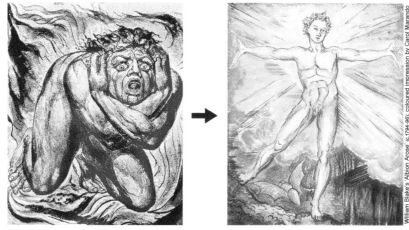

William Blake's *Cringing in Terror* (c.1794–96) left, and *Albion Arose* (c.1794–96) right

[62] While this therapising of our upset psychosis to the point where it no longer exists in the human race will, as I have emphasised, take a number of generations, the therapising actually begins from the moment we overcome the Deaf Effect and can access the redeeming understanding of our corrupted human condition. As Professor Prosen wrote, **'What Griffith is presenting is understanding of the source insecurity that the whole human race suffers from for having destroyed our species' innocent soul. It is a universal self-blame that his understanding at last provides healing insight into. All human behavior is saturated with that universal insecure, depressing state and resulting anger, egocentricity and alienation that has developed from it, but we finally have the compassionate foundation insight needed to dismantle all that 'upset'/psychosis. So the real psychotherapy of our collective and individual psychoses can begin'** (see FAQ 1.34).

[63] Yes, and it is such an immense relief for our minds to finally be able to make sense of all the suffering and seeming madness in human life, and of all that has happened in our own lives, that the minds of most people soak up the information; they absolutely guzzle it. As I describe in my book *The Shock of Change*, there is a great deal of stunned adjustment that our mind goes through when we first realise this information really does explain the human condition, but even when we are going through this shocked stage (where for example Ian Frazier, the author of the bestselling book *Great Plains*, said he was **'staggered into silence'** by what he was reading) the rapid soaking up of the information and its ameliorating effects typically still occurs. If you look at the 'daily ecstatic responses' slider under *THE Interview* at the top of www.humancondition.com you will see <u>endless comments by people who are finding immense healing relief from finally being able to understand the world and themselves</u>—such as **'The more I'm watching and reading, the more understanding I'm gaining'**, and **'Love this, learning more and more'**, and **'Understanding the human condition makes me feel free and happy'**, **'My attitude has changed, I'm not upset with myself anymore, I'm free of guilt and full of love'**, **'So wonderful to understand yourself and the whole world'**, **'Ever so grateful, it all finally makes sense. Gonna rebuild a new me'**, **'Once you get your head around it, it's light bulb time!'**, and **'I always knew that one day understanding of ourselves would save us from ourselves'**.

[64] Of course everyone, according to how much hurt to their soul they experienced growing up in the extremely psychologically upset world we are living in, will variously feel shocked, confronted and exposed by having our species' corrupted condition and their own corrupted condition revealed—this initial exposure being the cause of the Deaf Effect. As I point out in chapter 9:3 of *FREEDOM*, the arrival of understanding of the human condition represents exposure day or truth day or honesty day or transparency day or revelation day. In fact, it is the long-feared so-called **'judgment day'** referred to

in religious texts, although this **'judgment day'** is actually a day of compassionate understanding not a day of condemnation. Yes, as an anonymous Turkish poet once recognised, judgment day is **'Not the day of judgment but the day of understanding'** (Merle Severy, 'The World of Süleyman the Magnificent', *National Geographic*, Nov. 1987). <u>So while everyone will initially variously feel shocked, confronted and exposed by the revelation of the world's, and of their own, corrupted state, since the revelation is one of compassion, this pain from the shock and exposure, and the initial resistance and even anger it can cause towards the information, will pass and relief will be the final effect.</u> As Brian Carlton attested to in his interview with me that I included earlier, **'The end process, the revelation, if you like, is easy and reassuring and calming and self-accepting. Getting there is the difficult bit'.** Yes, as the saying goes, **'the truth hurts'**, but since it is the compassionate full truth that is being revealed, in time the **'hurt'** is replaced by immense relief and happiness. In chapter 9:7 of *FREEDOM* I present a detailed description of how everyone, including the more upset, can progress from feeling unbearably exposed by the explanation of the human condition, to feeling immensely relieved by it.

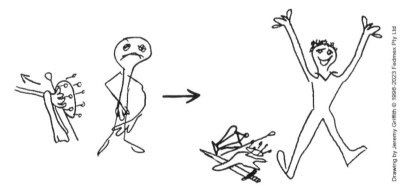

'Truth Day' or 'Honesty Day' or 'Revelation Day' or 'Exposure Day' or 'Judgment Day' ⟶ The human-race-saving and all-exciting Transformed Way of Living

[65] This natural healing of our upset that listening to and reading about this redeeming understanding of our corrupted condition produces can obviously also be supplemented and sped up by actively therapising our psychosis through the help and guidance of counselling. Now that humanity's corrupted condition has been explained and defended and the human race no longer has to live in denial of it to cope with it, and the human race can now 'come out of the closet' as it were about its now immensely corrupted state, therapising and healing our 2-million-year upset, soul-corrupted psychosis will be big business; it will be what many, many people will want to do. And to help with this demand, more and more counsellors will appear who are trained and skilled in using the redeeming understanding of the human condition to therapise psychosis. My book *Therapy For The Human Condition* is designed to initiate the development of this great new frontier that has opened up of the psychological rehabilitation of the human race.

Part 7. To save the world, the priority has to be the Transformed Way of Living, not therapy

[66] What now needs to be emphasised is that while many people will want to actively therapise their psychosis, the priority *always* has to be to take up the Transformed Way of Living because that alone is what can quickly bring the human race back from the brink of extinction from terminal levels of psychosis. Therapising upset is a process that takes time; in fact, as has been explained, to fully achieve it will take generations, and the reality is that, especially initially while this human-race-saving new world is getting underway, not a lot of therapy of upset will be possible. So at best it can initially only complement our adoption of the Transformed State. And it has to be remembered that everyone should not only want to take up the Transformed State because it saves the human

race, but also because, as I have described, it is the most incredibly relieving, exciting and satisfying state to be living in.

[67] I should also mention—and I talk about this at some length in my *Therapy* book—the human race has become so psychologically exhausted that even though the redeeming understanding of our corrupted condition needed to actually rehabilitate the human race hasn't been available until now, the need for psychological help has become so desperate that all manner of superficial attempts have and are being made to try to therapise psychological upset. This development of at least some superficial therapy has in fact become so desperately needed and so popular that it is one of the fastest growing industries in the world, with the Global Wellness Institute reporting in 2019 that **'Wellness is now a [US]\$4.2 trillion market that is growing nearly twice as fast as the global economy'** ('Good Health is Good Business', 13 Jun. 2019, Forbes. com; see www.wtmsources.com/300). Obviously if this superficial therapy is immensely popular, the *real* therapy that is now available is going to become *incredibly* popular, but again everyone needs to prioritise adopting the Transformed State because it frees us from practising the *now unnecessarily* psychologically upsetting, soul-destroying, older-generations-exhausting, younger-generations-crippling, competitive, selfish and aggressive way of living and by so doing hauls the human race back from the brink of terminal psychosis and extinction.

[68] So of course, it follows that with the real therapy of our psychologically upset lives now possible, there is going to be an immense hunger for it—'Why stay living with horribly debilitating and deadening psychosis when you have the means to at least begin healing it?' And it does make sense to heal our psychosis sufficiently for us to become at least to some degree functional, but, I stress again, focusing on therapising our upset can become a *selfish* preoccupation when THE PRIORITY IS TO TAKE UP THE TRANSFORMED WAY OF LIVING. So everyone has to temper their desire to therapise their personal psychosis with the human race's need for everyone to *selflessly* adopt the Transformed State or Way of Living.

[69]I drew this picture to warn against exploiting the insights we have gained into human behaviour to give yourself an 'edge' and make yourself even more successful in the old power and glory, ego-castle-building world, rather than focusing on supporting the new world, but this 'pocketing the win', as we in the WTM call it, also applies to the danger of focusing on rehabilitating your psychosis while avoiding taking up the Transformed State.

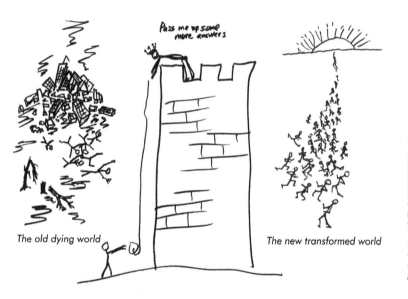

Pass me up some more answers

The old dying world

The new transformed world

Drawing by Jeremy Griffith © 1996-2023 Fedmex Pty Ltd

[70]So while therapy *is* going to be a huge business because everyone will want to and need to heal their psychosis to at least some degree, the infinitely bigger business *has to be, if the world is to be saved*, to take up the Transformed Way of Living—and it *will be* once it catches on because it is so absolutely incredibly relieving and exciting to be effectively free of the torturous and

dead human-condition-stricken existence. <u>NO MORE FOCUS ON SUPER CARS, OR BETTER UMBRELLAS, OR WAYS TO WIN FOOTBALL GAMES, JUST ON HOW TO GET FREE OF THE HELL ON EARTH OF THE HUMAN CONDITION—BECAUSE NOW AT LAST WE CAN!</u>

Part 8. The two parts to the transformation of the human race

[71] So there are two parts to the transformation of the human race: the Transformed Way of Living, and the therapy for our corrupted condition.

[72] For more on the Transformed Way of Living we suggest you now watch WTM founding member <u>Tony Gowing</u>, who is the

St Paul of the Transformed Way of Living, the most wonderful teacher and promoter of it, present his account of the Transformed Way of Living.

[73] Following Tony's presentation we suggest you watch the inspiring video of the Akritidis family from WTM Melbourne describing how being able to understand the human condition has brought incredible relief and therapy to their lives, as it can for everyone's life.

[74] And following my, Tony's and the Akritidis's videos—which are all on our Transformation page at www.humancondition.com/transformation—you will see there further wonderful examples of, and instructions about, those two parts of humanity's transformation.

[75] Also, the transcript of my, Tony's and the Akritidis's videos are all presented in [this] *The Great Transformation* booklet, which is freely available on our website, or you can purchase it from book shops like Amazon.

[76] **And remember that the best way to help transform the world and yourself is to become involved in the World Transformation Movement**—visit our Community page at www.humancondition.com/community, and our 'How to Help' page at www.humancondition.com/how-to-help.

Tony Gowing's presentation

Part 9. Tony Gowing describes how the Transformed Way of Living brings about the most fabulous transformation of everyone's life

Tony Gowing giving his presentation in *The Great Transformation*, 2023

Jeremy Griffith's introduction to Anthony (Tony) Gowing

[77] **Jeremy**: Welcome everybody to Tony Gowing's presentation about the magnificence of the Transformed Way of Living.

[78] Just to introduce Tony: Tony is a talent, I think he got the elephants over the Alps for Hannibal, and he swum with the river dolphins in the Amazon, and I think you lived with the gorillas, eating giant celery, in Rwanda there for six months or something Tone, is that right?! [Laughter]

[79] **Tony**: Well, getting the elephants over the Alps was the hard bit! [Laughter]

[80] **Jeremy**: Anyway, Tone could have done those things, but actually what he did do, what he has done, he's a country boy who turned up at the World Transformation Movement I think about 17 years ago now to make sure this understanding of the human condition reaches the world. He's an absolute super weapon of talent; he taught himself to write computer coding, to handle marketing, basically anything and everything—so wherever there's the greatest need that's where you'll find Tony.

[81] Above all, Tony is the St Paul of our movement, your guide to becoming transformed, so please listen closely to the best help you could ever wish for in learning how this understanding of the human condition is able to transform your life and save the world. So Tony, I'll leave it to you.

[82] **Tony**: Thanks very much Jeremy.

The magnificence of the Transformed Way of Living

[83] Thanks again Jeremy. I'm totally embarrassed by what you've said about me because I'm just nothing in all of this. Look, it's actually very simple: the World Transformation Movement [WTM], with the understanding of the human condition it supports, is the most important and wonderful organisation on Earth—and I just feel like I'm the luckiest person alive to be able to play any kind of a part in bringing this information to the world.

[84] And Jeremy is the most generous, most uniquely gifted, most sensitive, truly empathetic, honest, and insightful—and courageous—person that anyone could hope to meet. You can absolutely believe me on that! Nothing he ever says or does ever disappoints you.

[85] The main thing I've learnt from Jeremy is that this explanation of the human condition is the most important thing that is happening in the world by a million miles. And I do want to say that every part of our insecure, human-condition-afflicted selves can't help but want to block this information from seeing the light

of day, but the absolute opposite has to happen where we live in support of this understanding—because it's the only thing that can save the world. And that's what I love most about Jeremy, because he just lives to save the world in every breath he takes, and all I want to do is emulate that. He's shown me that I, and we all, can live completely selflessly like he does in support of the dignifying truth we now finally have for our corrupted condition.

[86] So I'm just here to help save the world because supporting this understanding of the human condition IS the only way we can!

[87] Now, the first thing I absolutely want to and absolutely need to do is replay this short extract from Jeremy's presentation which summarises <u>the essential benefit</u> of finally having the redeeming explanation of the human condition. <u>So this is the key information that makes a whole new world for us humans possible</u> [see paragraphs 39-41]:

"While our species' psychological rehabilitation will take a number of generations, what is so spectacularly wonderful is that <u>having the redeeming understanding of our fundamental goodness immediately obsoletes our old artificial ways of defending ourselves against the implication that our corrupted condition meant we are bad and unworthy</u>. Remember in *THE Interview* that I explained using the Adam Stork analogy how when we were unjustly criticised by our instincts for defying them and managing our life from a basis of understanding, that the only ways we could defend ourselves against our instincts' criticism was to <u>prove</u> that we weren't bad by competitively winning as much power, fame, fortune and glory as we could, and by angrily <u>attacking</u> the implication that we were bad, and by <u>blocking out</u> from our minds that implied condemnation. Well, now that we have found the *real* defence for our corrupted condition of the actual understanding of why we are good and not bad, those old *artificial* <u>egocentric</u>, <u>angry</u> and <u>alienated</u>

ways of defending ourselves are necessarily obsoleted. Those old defences have done their job and are no longer needed. Indeed, now that we have the *real* defence for our corrupted condition of the 'instinct vs intellect' biological explanation for why we corrupted ourselves, and therefore why we are actually good and not bad, it would be completely irresponsible given the plight of the world to continue using the now obsoleted, and thus now unnecessarily destructive, old *artificial* angry, egocentric and alienated ways of defending ourselves! With the real defence for our corrupted condition found, everyone can, and now must if we are to save the human race, abandon our old artificial ways of maintaining their sense of self-worth, and instead direct all our abilities and energies to supporting the redeeming understanding of the human condition that we now have and to adopting the cooperative, selfless and loving new way of living that it has made possible; indeed, that it has revealed we have no reason not to take up. We let go of our old, now obsoleted, selfish preoccupation with winning power, fame, fortune and glory as the way to sustain our sense of self-worth, and instead focus our mind on living for and through the fabulous cooperative, selfless and loving new potential that has opened up for the human race now that understanding of our corrupted human condition has been found and our soul/instinct and intellect are reconciled. Everyone now can and has to change from— be transformed from—being servants of our egos to being servants of humanity. We *had to* defensively defy our instincts to find understanding, ultimately self-understanding, understanding of why we corrupted our instinctive soul, so our egocentric defensive system was necessary, but now it no longer is. And, gloriously, what happens when we give up our old angry, egocentric and alienated way of living and take up this new Transformed Way of Living where we live in support of the understanding of the human condition is <u>we discover a freedom we have only ever dreamed of where we are no longer preoccupied justifying ourselves and proving our worth every minute of the day, as we actually *have* been every minute of the day, and as a result are finally able to access all the true beauty of our lives, of those around us, and of every living thing</u>. The shackles of the responsibility we have had of having to continue supporting and participating in humanity's immensely necessary and immensely heroic but at the same time immensely upsetting, soul-corrupting search for the redeeming understanding of why we defied our instincts fall away and <u>a whole new world that is effectively free of the agony of the human condition opens up for us. Even though we are not yet free of the psychologically upset state of our personal corrupted condition, we are *effectively* free of it, our lives are effectively transformed, because it is no longer the focus of our minds</u>. That is the seemingly magic <u>immediate</u> benefit of having the redeeming biological understanding of the human condition: we all—Baby Boomers, X-gen'ers, Y/Millennials, Z-gen'ers and Alpha-gen'ers—are <u>suddenly</u> free to live our lives in support of a non-competitive, non-selfish, non-aggressive and non-human-corrupted-condition-denying, peaceful and truthful, human-race-saving, cooperative, selfless and loving way of living that is effectively free of the agony of the human condition. <u>So this is how we are quickly able to bring the human race back from the brink of extinction from terminal levels of psychosis</u>."

[88] <u>So there Jeremy has given us all, in the clearest possible way, the reason for, and the benefits of, the fabulous Transformed Way of Living that understanding of the human condition has made possible, and is the way of living we in the WTM support and promote.</u>

[89] Shortly, I'll talk about the difficulty most people can initially have taking up the Transformed Way of Living where you let go of your now obsoleted power, fame, fortune and glory ways of validating yourself, but I have to begin—because it's so incredible—by telling you just how relieving and special it is to be able to live free of the agony of the human condition in the Transformed Lifeforce State (TLS), which is what we in the WTM also call the Transformed Way of Living—because you do turn into an absolute force for life when you take up the Transformed Life-force State!

[90] As everyone who has overcome the Deaf Effect and been able to access and appreciate Jeremy Griffith's explanation will know, the ability it gives you to understand every aspect of human life, including yourself, is absolutely drop-dead-with-relief-and-excitement, breathtakingly fantastic! The thousands of ecstatic responses under *THE Interview* on the WTM's home page reveal this immense relief and excitement—and gratitude—of being able to make sense of human existence, and know that the human race actually has a path out of the horror situation it is now in, the extent and gravity of which Jeremy made very clear in Part 3 of his presentation. So, once you get through the Deaf Effect, relief and excitement is the main effect of being able to make sense of everything.

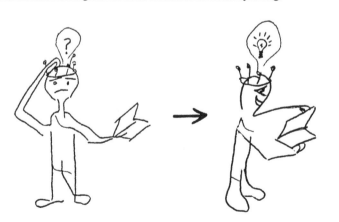

Drawing by Jeremy Griffith © 1996-2023 Fedmex Pty Ltd

Perseverance enables progression from being 'deaf'
to 'hearing' explanation of the human condition

Living in a world without answers, Tony at age 20, with his dog Basil in 2000

[91]And this information really *does* make sense of everything! What it has done for me is incredible. In the world before this explanation for me there were no answers, there was no meaning, no direction, no real understanding—I had no real idea what to do in the world, no framework of reference, no idea about the meaning of existence at all, in fact. Like almost every person, as an adolescent I had no choice but to 'resign' myself to blocking out the unbearably depressing truth of my and the human race's corrupted condition, and instead pretend life was fine and commit myself to just seeking reinforcement. [The process of Resignation is explained in Freedom Essay 30.] And so I honed my own talents of playing sport and striving for financial success or 'doing well' in my chosen career, but underneath all of that I knew that my life was a desperate, pain and stress-filled, dysfunctional mess. But now I have complete

understanding of human life. I know the good reason why the human race became corrupted, why we destroyed our loving soul. Yes, at the heart of all this amazing understanding, I'm able to understand that despite all appearances to the contrary, we humans aren't the outcasts, the baddies, the horrors, the downright monsters of planet Earth we have always worried we might be. I know that there is, in fact, tremendous purpose and meaning underlying everything in the world. So I know now that humans have been on this most wonderful journey of love and courage, and why it has taken such a toll on our species and our planet. I know now why we are the way we are, and why the world has been so mean and full of pain.

[92] And the wonder and relief of all this understanding is endless. Where everything was just so desperate, disappointing, meaningless, hopeless, depressing, tiring, hurtful and false—everything, every situation, every person, everything now is just enthusiasm, love, peace, relief, happiness and excitement. With the human condition at last resolved and our existence made sense of, everything can now be fixed and brought back to life.

[93] So it is beyond description how wonderful it is to be able to understand yourself and the world—and, as Jeremy has just explained, the logical outcome of this redeeming understanding of ourselves is that there can now be a wondrous change of heart in every single human; that I and every human can immediately make the change from being completely consumed by an incredibly insecure, mad, terrified and obsessively egocentric and selfish mindset, to a completely 100% secure person living out an all-meaningful, wildly exciting existence dedicated to helping make this change from darkness and pain to brilliant light and an all-understanding state of freedom from the human condition. And as this understanding grows and grows, it just becomes more and more obvious how obsoleted our old power, fame, fortune and glory way of justifying ourselves is. The more the understanding enables you to see through

what's been going on in your own life and in the world—how dead, horrible and totally and utterly barren, and (now) meaningless it is—the more attractive the Transformed Way of Living becomes where you are able to leave all that traumatised and now destructive behaviour and way of living behind. The transformation that this relieving, makes-sense-of-everything understanding of our corrupted human condition offers for our lives and for the whole world is truly awesome!

The human-race-saving and all-exciting Transformed Lifeforce State

[94] And so the Transformed State where you focus your mind not on making yourself a legend anymore but on living for a world free of the horror of the human condition becomes a no-brainer, a wonderful, wonderful, peaceful, satisfying, relieving thing to do!

[95] There's just no contest between the true meaning and radiance of what you will be doing, the scale of what you can be part of, the unfathomable significance of your life living for this information, as opposed to living for a new marble kitchen bench top, or a new car, or a promotion at work, whatever!

[96] So that's the first point I want to make, that I just can't wait for the whole world to experience what it's like to be free of the

relentless, manic, obsessive, dishonest, tyrannical desperation to prove ourselves, which is in truth what our lives have been like living under the duress of the human condition—and the unbelievable feeling of relief and exhilaration of living free of that in loving service of a whole new life of freedom from the agony of the human condition for the whole human race!

The utterly magnificent life living free of the agony of the
human condition in the warm healing light of understanding

[97] We can wake from the nightmare that humanity has had to endure while it searched for this redeeming understanding of our species' corrupted condition, and live our lives as part of the most wonderful, world-saving, all-suffering-ending, all-loving new existence for us brave and heroic humans—absolutely 100% secure in the knowledge that every ounce of energy that we expend every minute of every day now is going into a completely meaningful and right direction.

[98] We don't have to guess or 'try' to be a good person, or hope we are doing the right thing, WE KNOW WE ARE because we can at last make sense of human existence. We know in our minds and hearts that the path forward now is all clear, and how wonderful is

that! Enthusiasm, aliveness and unbelievable energy pours through our whole being like warm sunlight. We can wake up from our human-condition-afflicted stupor, and leave forever our manic, intensely driven, exhausting preoccupation with proving ourselves, and constantly making sure we are feeling good about ourselves that we have HAD to live like until now.

Power, fortune, fame and glory had to sustain us until we found
real reinforcement, understanding.

[99] At this point you might be thinking that this is all sounding like the most 'New Age', utopian-seduced pile of away-with-the-pixies bullshit you have ever heard! And look, I know it's absolutely justified to think that—there have been so many false starts to a human-condition-free new world throughout human history that any talk of such a liberation is on the nose, it absolutely wreaks of delusion and even madness, so being a bit sickened and put off by what I have been saying is okay. But this is the amazing thing—what I have been saying is actually all true. This fabulous, dreamed-of great transformation of our lives from a human-condition-stricken state to a human-condition-free life is totally real—because we have actually finally found the fully understandable, first-principle-based, scientific, biological, human-race-rehabilitating explanation of our corrupted human condition that makes the transformation of our lives 100% legitimate, real and right!

[100] All that I am saying is totally verifiable, logical and rational! I know it's astonishing that this has finally happened, but it has happened! The efforts of everyone throughout the ages have finally led to the all-redeeming and all-relieving and all-healing understanding

of the human condition. It is like a miracle, but it is actually very real! We, the human race, are free to leave our upset, corrupted lives behind forever. God almighty, this IS incredible, but get used to it, because it's true!

[101] And I want to absolutely reiterate what Jeremy said in his presentation—that this Transformed Way of Living has *nothing* at all to do with the deluded, pseudo idealistic, no-understanding-of-the-human-condition, totally artificial and totally dangerous left-wing, socialist, new age, PC, 'woke' movement. As Jeremy fully explains in his brilliant booklet *Death by Dogma*, that is such a dangerous false start to a transformed world for the human race—one of the horrible false starts I was referring to that have discredited this real start to a transformed world that understanding of the human condition ACTUALLY makes possible. And again, you have the first-principle biological explanation of the human condition to verify that this IS the real start. There's no naive dreaming, or mindless dogmatic enforcement of an ideal world involved. This is all science based and driven.

[102] And as Jeremy also emphasised, this has nothing to do with religion where people defer to, and live through support of, the *embodiment* of the ideals in the form of a denial-free-thinking great prophet. This is about living in support of the *understanding* of our corrupted condition that actually makes a cooperative and loving ideal world possible. As Jeremy often says, this is the end of faith and belief and the beginning of knowing!

[103] With understanding of the human condition we are now able to see and implement the stunningly wonderful, GENUINE path home for humanity and for ourselves. It is so obvious and clear what to do now. We can truly live with purpose, freedom and joy. All of our old human-condition-afflicted pursuits can be left in the pile of rubble that they now represent. We know our embattled way of living used to be needed, but now it's no longer needed and it IS now meaningless, pointless, destructive rubble! That way of living brought us this far, but it's over now.

[104] So let's go, let's get the fuck out of the old dead world—let's dedicate our lives and minds and hearts to freeing the world and freeing ourselves from the hell on Earth that Jeremy truthfully described the human condition as being!

From dystopia to utopia!

[105] And living that way is the only way to show the rest of the world that the human condition is not scary anymore—by taking up the Transformed Way of Living we are embracing the truth of our corruption, we aren't fearfully defying it any more, and that is very best evidence that Jeremy's redeeming understanding has at last made the human condition safe. And the more relaxed we are with the human condition inside of ourselves, and the more we are able to be honest about it and accept it, the more empathetic we can be toward everyone else's suffering under the human condition, and so the more we can help them overcome their initial fear of the subject.

[106] Basically, we don't have to feel guilty a second longer, we don't have to manically push all our hurt and fears down, and hide it all, and lie and pretend, and live in hope anymore. What we have hoped

for is here, this is it! Our task now is to help others discover this understanding until it has reached every corner of the world. It will be our unbridled enthusiasm, clear sightedness, and selfless positivity that will build more and more momentum in ourselves, in our group of supporters, and ultimately take this amazing breakthrough to the rest of the world. So let's love the world back to life with Jeremy's magnificent understanding of the human condition, and bring an end to all the suffering, madness and desperation. Let's GO!

Coping with 'exposure day' or 'judgment day', and overcoming the 'Mexican Standoff'

[107] So that is how genuinely fabulous the Transformed State is—it is actually more wonderful than I can describe, and that is just the truth!

[108] What I now want to look at and help everyone with are TWO PARTICULAR DIFFICULTIES most people initially encounter once they overcome the Deaf Effect and appreciate the information and are on their way to taking up the Transformed Way of Living.

[109] The FIRST DIFFICULTY is having our own personal version of humanity's 2-million-year corrupted condition—which we have been coping with by living in complete denial of it—SUDDENLY EXPOSED by the arrival of the explanation of the human condition. As Jeremy described it in his presentation, this is 'exposure day' or 'truth day' or 'revelation day' or 'honesty day', or 'judgment day', which as Jeremy emphasised, is actually a time of compassionate understanding not condemning 'judgment'. Nevertheless, the sudden exposure of our corrupted condition cannot help but be a shock, and like all shocks, that has to be worked through.

'Exposure Day' or 'Judgment Day'

[110] Personally, I am chock-full of the corrupted human condition. I know every cell in my body is infected with the insecurity from being so corrupted, the suicidally depressing guilt and shame of it, which Jeremy's explanation has finally allowed us to let go of. At times I can visualise all this corruption in me and my historic fear of it as a thick black sticky substance that has slowly become more stagnant with age and the experiences of life. And this deep hurt and insecurity, which, at its core has been my fear of encountering the truth of my corrupted condition, has driven my dysfunction, driven my focus on myself, driven my competition with others, driven my egocentric need to fight back and try to prove I am a good and worthy and capable person. But as Jeremy has explained over and over again, the key piece of logic we all have to remind ourselves of—in fact, as I will explain, we have to forge a whole new highway in our brain around—is that we don't have to fear the truth of our corrupted condition anymore. We have the redeeming, 100% compassionate explanation of the 2-million-year corrupted state of the human condition that we can now accept the truth of, and just let

all our historic insecurities and resulting defensive behaviours go. In fact, as I'm about to explain, our feelings of fear, guilt, shame and embarrassment about our corrupted condition can now be completely flipped into feelings of immense pride, relief and joy!

[111] So this great dreamed-of breakthrough understanding of our corrupted human condition is naturally initially exposing and confronting, but, since we have understanding of what is happening when we feel this exposure, we can, with patience, not only cope with the exposure of our corrupted condition but achieve a state of dreamed-of complete release from our shame and guilt about it.

[112] In chapter 9:3 of *FREEDOM* Jeremy gives a full account of the 'judgment day' effect of having our corrupted condition exposed, and in chapter 9:7 he gives a detailed description of how everyone, including the more upset who have more psychological hurt to be exposed, can cope with this shock of exposure. Basically, with sufficient time to adjust everyone can not only cope with having their corrupted condition exposed, but be immensely relieved to be able to effectively live free of their corrupted condition by taking up the Transformed State. And as more people make the adjustment to the truth of their own and the whole human race's corrupted condition, and more people adopt the Transformed State, there will be more reassurance and support to help everyone cope with having their own and the human race's corrupted condition exposed.

Graphic by J. Griffith, M. Rowell and G. Salter © 2009 Fedmex Pty Ltd

[113] The SECOND DIFFICULTY in taking up the Transformed Way of Living, is that OUR ATTACHMENT to our old, now obsoleted, 'must-prove-my-worth', 'must-establish-that-I'm-good-not-bad', 'must-get-a-win-from-every-situation', power, fame, fortune and glory way of validating ourselves IS SO HABITUATED AND STRONG THAT MANY PEOPLE STRUGGLE TO LET GO OF THAT WAY OF LIVING and take up the Transformed Way of Living.

Our now baseless fear of exposure of our corrupted human condition

Resistance to letting go our now-obsoleted selfish power, fame, fortune and glory-seeking way of justifying our worth

The Transformed Lifeforce Way of Living

Drawing by Jeremy Griffith © 1996-2014 Fedmex Pty Ltd

[114] Again, it will get easier and easier to adopt the Transformed Way of Living as more and more people overcome the Deaf Effect and discover the power of this information to make sense of our lives, and from there get over feeling exposed by the understandings and discover just how legitimate, and necessary and relieving it is to be able to let go of our old, insecure, must-prove-my-worth, defensive behaviours and transform our lives to living in support of these human-race-saving understandings. HOWEVER, especially in the early stages of this great awakening of the human race from a 2-million-year long, traumatised, deep torpor, you can experience what we in the WTM call the 'MEXICAN STANDOFF'. This is where you know the information is true and that all the logic says you can and should let go of all your old artificial ways of validating yourself, but you have become so dependent on and attached to those ways of living that you find yourself unable to let them go.

[115] These reinforcements where we gain relief from the underlying insecurity we all carry by making ourselves feel good through winning power, fame, fortune or glory, and by blocking out the truth of our corrupted condition, and by attacking any implications that we are a bad person—these egocentricities, denials and angers, are all *artificial* reinforcements and coping mechanisms. As Jeremy summarised, the arrival of the *real* reinforcement of the actual explanation of why we are good and not bad, which is the 'instinct vs intellect' explanation of the human condition, obsoletes these *artificial* reinforcements—but having lived off these artificial reinforcements, it is natural to initially find it difficult to let them go. And so you find yourself in a Mexican Standoff where you can't deny that we now have the actual redeeming understanding of the human condition that obsoletes all those old artificial ways of justifying and defending ourselves, but you struggle to accept letting go of those old artificial defences that sustained and looked after us for so long.

Drawing by Jeremy Griffith © 2019 Fedmex Pty Ltd

Stuck in the Mexican Standoff

[116]To understand the solution to this problem of the Mexican Standoff it helps to really bottom out on just how extremely attached we have become to our old now obsoleted ways of validating and defending ourselves.

[117]It doesn't matter who you are, where you come from or what you've been doing in your life, the truth is that living with the insecurity about our self-worth that all humans carry as a result of our corrupted condition has meant every one of us has been spending our whole lives, every second of every day, totally preoccupied with fighting back against that underlying insecurity. We have had to build intricate facades that we curate with the utmost attention to detail to protect us from exposure of our seemingly unworthy, bad and evil corrupted condition that Jeremy has finally presented the redeeming explanation of. The truth is we humans have been completely dedicated to building and maintaining these facades, but because we've been living in denial of our corrupted condition to protect ourselves from unbearable exposure of it, we are hardly

aware that we have been totally focused on building and maintaining these protective facades.

Maintaining our facades

[118] We like to think we are doing all kinds of wonderful things like working, travelling, going to university, supporting a charity, being with family, children and friends, going to parties, etc, etc, but really the truth is we have just been using all these seemingly normal aspects of our lives as vehicles to carry out our objective of resisting the underlying insecurity that we aren't worthy beings.

[119] And the extremely confronting truth is that this preoccupation has meant we actually haven't been able to genuinely care about what we convince ourselves we have been caring about in these activities, namely selflessly caring about the wellbeing of others and of the world; we've actually only been selfishly caring about how we can use these activities to hold back the suicidally depressing fear that

our corrupted condition means we are bad, unworthy people. We are using these activities to bolster our self-esteem.

Selfishly making ourselves feel good

[120] I know what I've said can be difficult to hear and accept, but this selfish preoccupation is just a product of the diabolically horrible and desperate situation we humans have been living in where we have been unjustly condemned as evil beings when we actually aren't—and therefore how single-minded and courageous we have all had to be to continue living in that horrifically unjust situation!

[121] The reason for pointing this truth out is not to make ourselves feel guilty or bad but to help us be aware of it because <u>that awareness is what helps most in being able to let that preoccupation go now that we have the real defence of the understanding of our corrupted condition</u>.

[122] Our great obsession with validating ourselves, with artificially making ourselves feel we are worthy and good, shows how important all the ways we have developed to validate ourselves have been. <u>We have a seriously strong attachment to our 'old world wins', so when the logic says we should let them all go and adopt the Transformed State we find ourselves in a situation that is like two freight trains</u>

coming from opposite directions down a single track in a giant game
of chicken!

The logic that says give up your now redundant strategies colliding
with your habituated attachment to those redundant strategies

[123] And initially you won't even know these two sides are set on a
collision course. One part of you will love this information because
you can see how it explains everything, and you know that it can
and will transform the world, so you want to support it by taking
up the Transformed Way of Living, but at the same time, there is
another part of you that just can't cope with the information, that
it's just all too confronting and exposing of your corrupted self, and
too undermining and stifling of all your historic egocentric ways of
validating yourself!

[124] You will feel like you have been asked to capitulate, give up
trying to establish that you are a good and not a bad person, and
since you, like everyone else, have prided yourself on never giving
into the assertion that you are a bad, unworthy person, you are
determined to not having to seemingly give in to it now. You in
effect say, "You must be joking if you think I'm going to stop being
proud of all my success in holding at bay the implication that I'm
a bad, unworthy person, stop maintaining 'my trophy room', end
my focus on making myself a legend, stop working every second of
the day on proving I'm a good person, stop what I have been doing
all my life, let go of everything I have worked so hard to achieve,
turn myself into a weak failure in the world—you have got to be
joking if you think I am going to do that!"

[125]The wrestling match between the ways you have been validating yourself and the Transformed Way of Living where you let
all those ways of validating yourself go and live for and through
your support of a human-condition-resolved new world can be
extreme. In fact, it can be so extreme that you may try to resolve
it by pretending you have accepted letting go of your old power,
fame, fortune and glory ways of validating yourself. For example,
you might say, "I'm already being incredibly supportive of this
information, what more could I possibly be doing, the WTM is
lucky to have my support", or even "I need more help from the
WTM so I can be even more supportive".

Pretending to be living in support of the WTM

Drawing by Jeremy Griffith © 1996-2023 Fedmex Pty Ltd

[126]But such pretence at having let go of your old validating
structure will still leave you stranded in the Mexican Standoff. In
particular, you will never experience what happens when you take up
the Transformed State, which is that you will have such an incredible
freedom of thought, and such an incredible enthusiasm for life, and
such incredible excitement about what is possible for the world, and

be so full of initiatives and energy and commitment to the transformed new world, you will hardly have time to breathe—which is
how I feel all the time, and why I work so hard for this project all
the time; and, if you watch Jeremy's behaviour, you will see that
he is living with that energy and enthusiasm and amazing commitment all the time too. A pretend transformation and a real one are
a million miles apart! [At the end of Tony's presentation there is a
link to where you can read about Jeremy Griffith's incomparable
example of how to live for the new world.]

[127] Since what I have just said about the trap of our attachment
to your old system of reinforcement is so important I am going to
try to say it again even more forcefully. Everyone will try to both
support the new and maintain the old—you know, go to church on
Sunday and then make money and kick heads the rest of the week!
You accept that the human race can't go on the way it is going,
that the old world is horrible and destructive and selfish and dying
and perpetuating suffering, and that the new transformed world is
wonderful and selfless and radiant and integrative and nurturing and
sympathetic and empathetic, and that it is the only path forward for
the human race—yet what virtually everyone initially tries to do is
(as a quote from Jeremy that I'll include shortly points out) try to fit
the new world into our old world lives. We use the understanding
of the human condition to defend our upset, we go on about how
upset we are and how that upset is now all defended; we even use
the insight the understandings gives us to increase our 'old world
wins'. We try to pretend we've always loved birds and nature and
were soulful, that we've always loved children and been nurturing.
We try to tell everyone how much the information has helped our
lives and, as I mentioned, how much we support the WTM; we'll
look on at everyone and point out how upset they are and silly and
crazy, how left-wing and off-track others are, and how we were
really genuinely right-wing, etc, etc. But all this doesn't work, the
old world and the new world don't mesh, we're still stuck in the
Mexican Standoff!

Still stuck in the Mexican Standoff!

Drawing by Jeremy Griffith © 1991 Fedmex Pty Ltd

[128] So when you're still stuck in the Mexican Standoff you can think you're living for the human-condition-resolved new world when you actually aren't; you're still firmly holding onto your old validation structure.

[129] Jeremy gives a very interesting illustration of the difficulty of the Mexican Standoff in paragraph 50 of his *The Shock of Change* video/booklet. While emphasising that the Transformed Way Of Living is not a religion, he points out that both the Transformed Way of Living and living in support of a prophet in religion do both involve letting go of your preoccupation with your corrupted condition. He then points out that, in the case of Christianity, Christ's 12 disciples, who were his first followers, didn't properly see how the faith that Christ was introducing worked. They venerated and worshipped Christ, but that was not the point—the real point of Christianity is to let go your embattled, overly-upset, self-preoccupied way of living and instead defer to and live through your support of Christ [see the explanation of Christ in Freedom Essay 39]. Jeremy then made the interesting observation that I wasn't aware of, which is that just as people resist letting go their upset way of living and taking up the Transformed State where you live in support of the redeeming understanding of ourselves, so the disciples also resisted letting go of their upset way of living and deferring to and living in support of Christ, actually complaining that **'This is a hard teaching. Who can accept it?'** (John 6:60). So

they saw it as **'hard teaching'**, and didn't want to **'accept it'**. As Jeremy then explains, it was actually <u>St Paul</u>, who came along afterwards (and who I'll talk more about shortly), who realised the immense 'fall off your donkey' relief that living in support of Christ rather than in the way your corrupted condition wanted you to live, was how Christianity works. The disciples loved the soundness of Christ, just as people love the sound understandings of the human condition, but it is living in support of the understanding of the human condition that transforms your life and saves humankind.

[130] Unless you take up the Transformed Way Of Living you are not making proper use of being able to understand the human condition. <u>Basically, you are still not seeing the situation you are in clearly.</u> You are just seeing it vaguely from a position where your old focus on validating yourself still holds sway—the "You want me to change, you must be kidding, I'm not a weak capitulator, forget it, now what I was doing"—which is the same old have-to-prove-you're-good-and-not-bad road you have been forcing yourself along all your life. <u>To make the change from your obsoleted old life to the new Transformed Way of Living you have to see your situation clearly, and through doing that realise and accept that what you have to do is change the focus of your mind. If you are still mentally framed up supporting your old form of reinforcement you will be stuck wrestling with wanting to maintain that, whereas you have to change to being mentally framed up to focus forward on supporting the fabulous new potential for the human race. The two ways of thinking are INCOMPATIBLE, MUTUALLY EXCLUSIVE, so you leave one alone, never look back at it, and lock onto the new validation system of living for and through supporting a human-condition-free new world for the human race. You have to put yourself on the spot, face your situation squarely; in the old religious terminology, you can't serve 'two gods', you can't maintain your old selfish focus and take up the selfless, humanity-focused Transformed Way of Living at the same time—it's one or the other!</u>

¹³¹ So there *is* a path through the Mexican Standoff, and that is for your mind to have the right orientation, which is to completely leave behind and forget your old redundant reinforcement system and instead focus on living through supporting a world free of the horror of the human condition—which we absolutely have to do, because if we don't the human race will perish through terminal levels of psychosis, and the point of no return is genuinely only a few short decades away; and if you want to imagine what terminal levels of psychosis looks like, it is 100% of the human race suffering extreme autism—a degree of paralysis, agony and distress that is so terrible it is unthinkable—so honestly, everyone HAS TO hear about this information and take up the Transformed Way of Living!

THE DEATH OF HUMANITY

¹³² Yes, people caught in this no-mans-land of realising the unfathomable importance of these explanations, but allowing themselves to be wedded to their historic defences, is actually the ultimate state of wrongness, the ultimate obscenity. Even though wanting to genuinely support this information is what we know we want to and should do, attachment to your old validating way of living makes doing that impossible. In fact, remaining in that position without clear awareness of it can build and build and build, and cause huge levels of distress, and if left unchecked it can even force you back into living in the old cave of denial, and even worse, make you attack the information and the WTM [read more in Freedom Essay 56: *Why have there been ferocious attacks on the WTM*]. So this is

why all this clear awareness of what is happening in you is very important.

Futilely attacking the truth

Drawing by Jeremy Griffith © 2018 Fedmex Pty Ltd

[133] So yes, it really is the 'ultimate obscenity' to hang onto your old, now completely unnecessary and now world-destroying ways of validating yourself. That old way of living was necessary but it no longer is, it's done its job, it's now finished with and immensely destructive to continue with it, so just forget it. And once you clearly see and accept that truth you will find you actually *can* let that now obsoleted and destructive way of living go and take up the Transformed Way of Living where you live for and through supporting the new human-condition-resolved world!

[134] And again—and most significantly and importantly—when you let go of your old preoccupation with trying to artificially validate yourself every minute of every day, which is what you have been doing, you will discover an absolutely incredible freedom you didn't dream could be possible. And this will happen because the immense burden of guilt about being corrupted that has actually been weighing you down, and the whole human race down for 2 million years, will be lifted from your shoulders—which is actually how you become a Transformed Life-force, a person living effectively free of the burden of the human condition—and you will feel all the relief, excitement

and enthusiasm that I described at the beginning of my presentation. Taking up the Transformed State saves the human race, that's its benefit to humanity, but it's fabulous benefit to you is that you will feel a 50-tonne weight lifted off your shoulders and experience a state of freedom and exhilaration and excitement we humans have never been able to allow ourselves to think could exist while we were having to participate in humanity's immensely upsetting, heroic battle to find the redeeming understanding of the human condition!

[135] Yes, you can't experience the fabulous new while you are still worshipping at the altar of the dead-as-door-nails old!

St Paul falling off his donkey and going blind with ecstatic relief
after he let go of his struggle with the human condition

[136] In paragraphs 1198-1199 of his book *FREEDOM*, Jeremy explains how when St Paul gave up his insecure, destructive battle to prove he is a legend by deferring to Christ he was overcome with such relief he was metaphorically struck blind for three days and fell off his donkey, and Jeremy uses what happened to St Paul to tell us how even more justified and relieving it is now to be able to

let go of our struggle with the human condition—and I'm here to tell you how true that is! When you 'get' this, when you actually let go of the battle, you will metaphorically go blind with relief for not just three days but forever and ever, and you'll fall off the back of not just one donkey but millions of the long-eared little fellas! Understanding of the human condition has the ability to completely and permanently free every human on Earth from the agony of the human condition. <u>We are *all* free now—you and everyone else just have to realise that and take your freedom!</u>

[137] I should mention a clarification Jeremy makes about the Transformed Way of Living in paragraph 20 of *The Shock of Change*, which is that <u>the focus in leaving the old world of artificial reinforcement isn't on giving up your possessions, or walking the streets in sackcloth, in self-denial and servitude.</u> We're talking about a change of mindset that can have an effect on your priorities, which can affect your choice of possessions and so forth, but the focus isn't on self-deprivation.

[138] <u>The absolute best description of how to not try to serve 'two gods' of our old selfish way of validating ourselves and the new selfless Transformed State, but instead letting the former go, is this passage from Jeremy in Video/Freedom Essay 33.</u>

"What happens is you don't actually try to get this understanding of the human condition to mesh with your power and glory way of living. You don't try to get one to accommodate the other, which is actually what you've been doing. That's why you're at odds with this transformation. Even the words 'at odds' suggest that there's a war between the two. That's the mistake you're making because <u>what you do is you actually leave that whole wrestling match completely, and go to another place that's free of that wrestling match</u>. The mistake you've been making is wrestling with this, trying to get the Transformed State to marry, or coexist with, your old way of sustaining yourself. <u>But in fact</u>

they're incompatible, they can't coexist, that's the thing you're missing. You give up—even saying 'give up' is inferring that you're still involved with that battle—you just leave that whole war alone and you go and live in another place. Trying to get one to accommodate the other was completely wrong. That's the mistake. You don't, you just leave that whole wrestling match alone. And once you understand that, it makes a world of difference. You just leave that battle as is. The Transformed State has nothing to do with it; you go and live in a place that's free of that battle. And as I'll now explain, you're not only free of the wrestling match, you go and live for the project, live for getting this information to the world, and that sustains you, that's what you live off in this fabulous state free of that deadening egocentric existence."

'You just leave that whole war alone and you go and live in another place.'

[139] That whole presentation in Video/Freedom Essay 33 by Jeremy is so helpful—and you can learn much more about the Mexican Standoff and how to overcome it in FAQ 1.23, and in Jeremy's video/booklet *The Shock of Change*, and especially in chapter 9 of *FREEDOM*.

How absolutely wonderful this Transformed Way of Living is

[140] So going back to what I said at the beginning, just imagine when you can truly give yourself with all your heart, soul and mind to freeing the human race from the human condition. You don't have to think about or worry about who you are, or what you are doing — you know what you are doing: you are living for the understanding that saves all the children on Earth from ever having to resign, to die inside themselves from having to endure the human condition, basically for a future that is kind and loving. You are able to be with others and not have to compete or feel like you don't understand them, or feel that they don't understand you. You don't have to drive yourself day in and day out to keep busy, to not think, or to project the best possible impression of yourself. We will genuinely love ourselves, and we will genuinely love and understand each other. We will be living in harmony with the world, with nature, with all the animals and plants, not as destructive outcasts anymore. All the problems on Earth will no longer be insoluble.

Peace On Earth

Drawing by Jeremy Griffith © 1996 Fedmex Pty Ltd

[141] It is just so beautiful to think about the future and to know that we can participate in it as much as we want to, and the more we participate the better we will feel, and the sooner the world will be safe. <u>Our job is to build the wonderful island of sanity that this fabulous understanding creates in us compared to the sea of madness everywhere else in the world</u>. So we just take up any task, no matter how small, something that will help build the momentum in any way—write a post or comment on the WTM's Facebook Group, send an email or even a hardcopy of *THE Interview* or *FREEDOM* to a thought leader, give a dollar to the advertising campaign, clean up our own human-condition-afflicted lives [<u>see our 'How to help' page at www.humancondition.com/how-to-help</u>]. The more centred we become on our task, the more generous to others and humanity we can be, and the more everyone will notice and ask what the difference is. We now have the ultimate meaning in our lives to live for, and the more we live that meaning, allow it into our lives, the more momentum, happiness, freedom we are helping to build. And we don't have to feel insecure or guilty for feeling wonderful because it's not a lie, we won't be pretending, we won't be putting on a show—this will be the most real thing we have ever been part of in our lives. To start with it might feel a bit strange because it's so new, but soon it won't feel strange, it will just be bliss day in and day out. What a complete change that is, the great **'change of heart'** that Sir James Darling trained Jeremy to give to us.

[142] Before finishing I would like to give credit to <u>Annie Williams</u> who was the inspiration for my transformation—I remember saying to myself, 'I want some of that freedom and excitement that she has found!' You might like to watch her absolutely wonderful Transformation Affirmation at www.humancondition.com/annie-williams-affirmation where you will see she confirms everything I've been saying. Which makes me think how true it is what Sir Laurens van der Post said (which Jeremy quoted in his book *How Laurens van der Post Saved The World*) about women initially being more able than men to acknowledge a denial-free, truthful-thinking

prophet: **'Not by the men, but by the women who flock to him and their obedience, shall you first know the true prophet'** (*The Heart of the Hunter*, 1961, p.131 of 233). Yes, and men's greater attachment to their egocentric power and glory defenses means they tend to be slower than women in taking up the Transformed Way of Living—which does mean <u>women have a big role to play leading humanity home to freedom from the human condition</u>.

Annie Williams presenting her Transformation Affirmation in 2010

[143] So I'm going to finish by reading this wonderful anticipation of a Transformed State-led, human-condition-free world from the great denial-free thinking prophet Joel, who Jeremy quotes in paragraph 1259 of *FREEDOM*: **'Like dawn spreading across the mountains a large and mighty army comes, such as never was of old nor ever will be in ages to come... Before them the land is like the garden of Eden, behind them, a desert waste— nothing escapes them. They have the appearance of horses; they gallop along like cavalry. With a noise like that of chariots...like a mighty army drawn up for battle. At the sight of them, nations are in anguish; every face turns pale.** [The reconciling truth is shockingly confronting and exposing at first, but those who have progressed past the shock stage are filled with excitement about being transformed and having the capacity to end human suffering and the

devastation happening on Earth.] **They charge like warriors; they scale walls like soldiers. They all march in line, not swerving from their course. They do not jostle each other** [Joel 2]…[and] **In that day the mountains will drip new wine, and the hills will flow with milk; all the ravines…will run with water** [Joel 3].'

[144] Yes, we all **'march in line, not swerving from'** our **'course'**, and all together with no one **'jostl**[ing] **each other'**. And as I said earlier, the more people that discover this explanation of the human condition, and take up the Transformed Way of Living, the easier and faster will be the human-race-liberated **'dawn spreading across the mountains'** of the world. So let's go, let's get out of this hell on Earth of the human condition!

[145] I suggest you now watch the video of the Akritidis family of WTM Melbourne describing the therapy they have derived from being able to understand the human condition, and then see further wonderful examples of, and instructions about, humanity's transformation on our Transformation page at www.humancondition.com/transformation.

[146] Also, the transcript of Jeremy's, my and the Akritidis's videos are all presented in [this] *The Great Transformation* booklet, which is freely available on our website, or you can purchase it from book shops like Amazon.

[147] **And remember that the best way to help transform the world and yourself is to become involved in the World Transformation Movement**—visit our Community page at www.humancondition.com/community, and our 'How to Help' page at www.humancondition.com/how-to-help.

The Akritidis's presentation

Part 10. The Akritidis family demonstrates how being able to understand the human condition is able to therapise our lives

Jeremy Griffith introduces the Akritidis family

[148] **Jeremy Griffith**: In my presentation I mentioned the endless number of 'daily ecstatic responses' in the slider under *THE Interview* at the top of www.humancondition.com that attest to the healing relief people are experiencing from being able to understand the world and themselves—such as **'Love this, learning more and more'**, and **'it's light bulb time, everything finally makes sense!'**. Well, the following 2020 video of members of the Akritidis family in Melbourne, Australia—all of whom are part of the WTM Melbourne Centre (WTMMelbourne.com)—provides a wonderful example of how incredibly relieving, reconciling and healing being able to understand the human condition is.

[149] You will see how the father has been able to compassionately understand, and therefore be honest about, his extremely egocentric behaviour and how psychologically crushing it has been of everyone (you can read about the 'power addicted' state in chapter 8:16D of *FREEDOM*). And you will see how relieving the honest understanding we now have about the relationship between men and women (which you can read about in chapter 8:11B of *FREEDOM*) has been for the women in the family. And you will see how the younger members of the family are so relieved to be able to understand why it has been so difficult for young people to cope with the soul-destroyed, seemingly mad world we live in. (You can read more about the relief that is now available for young people in my booklet *Our Meaning*.) The relief the family—and everyone now—can experience from finally being able to understand the human condition just goes on and on!

The Akritidis family, Dec. 2019
L to R: Ari, Katerina, Alex, Nicoletta, Chris, Nikola Tsivoglu, Desi

The Akritidis family presentation

[150] **Ari Akritidis**: [Building surveyor & fire safety engineer] I'm Ari Akritidis. I came across the WTM about 15 years ago through my youngest brother, Sam. He read the book *A Species In Denial* (one of Jeremy's earlier books) and shared it with me in around 2005. It took a while for me to really get my head around the information. But eventually it's just ecstasy—when you read and listen with an open mind, it's ecstasy.

[151] On a personal level, the information has helped me massively; it's helped me in my relationship with my wife [Desi], it's helped me in my relationship with my children. I sympathise with my kids and every human that's lost touch with their child-self, because we had to, and that includes my own children; I had to realise that they've gone through a process of Resignation that was largely because of my behaviour—so my compassion for them and for all children today is beyond anything that was possible pre-understanding. [Resignation is the psychological process whereby adolescents

wrestle with and 'resign' to the horror of the human condition, see Freedom Essay 30].

[152] So as a dad and a husband: my wife and I, like all couples, we fight, we love each other. We've been married 27 years, but we fight because we don't understand each other. Men and women are different. And Jeremy explains it; he explains *so* succinctly the different strategies we had to adopt as men and women to deal with the human condition. So I have compassion for my wife, I understand her journey, both on an individual and at a gender level. And she can understand me, which is just fantastic! [The difference between men and women is explained in chapter 8:11B of *FREEDOM*.]

[153] Before I came across this information, I now realise that I was a 'power addict', what we would refer to in the old world as a control freak, with an addiction to power at a subconscious level [the 'power addicted' state is explained in chapter 8:16D of *FREEDOM*]. What I needed to realise was how much that power was important to me to reinforce my own goodness, because I didn't know if I was good. There's a part of me that was wrestling with this underlying question: "Am I good or am I bad?" It's there, it's festering below the surface and that's what feeds your behaviour. And to break free of that, to be able to see that clearly now, can only be done when you're understood, when you understand yourself. Certainly, being able to see that now and appreciate the necessity of that strategy has been gold for me, it's absolutely gold.

[154] You can look at yourself, you can rat on yourself, you can laugh at yourself, because you're completely defended and you're a hero.

[155] This information will completely liberate everybody and free you of all of the uncertainty. And it's not describable—our vocabulary unfortunately hasn't caught up with the excitement that this information brings. Jeremy's explanations are more meaningful than any brain can possibly imagine. We actually now have a pathway

to healing! It's the greatest, the greatest gift anybody could have given us.

[156] **Desi Akritidis**: I believe I never would have been interested in embracing the information had it not been for the kids, because for me I felt "I don't need it, it's not going to help me"; I didn't understand it. So I learnt a lot initially through conversations; I was very lucky with Sam, my brother-in-law, as a trusted person, so obviously over the years I learned a lot through him and I've learnt a lot through my eldest son, Chris.

[157] **Chris Akritidis**: [Accredited sports nutritionist & personal trainer] I'm 22 and I'm down in Melbourne. My sibling Nicoletta here is 17, and my brother [Alex] is 18, my girlfriend [Nikola] is 21, and on the other screen you will see my other sister [Katarina, who is also 17; she and Nicoletta are twins], so we're all quite young and it's an interesting time for us because we have information and we can see an honesty well beyond our years.

[158] Being an eldest son, it was incredibly important for me to understand my own father's egocentricity because growing up as a son I always wanted dad's love, and as I got older it became quite combative between me and my father, because you start to retaliate. And really, I started to see in my dad things I didn't like about myself, and it was only again through understanding the human condition within myself that it dissipated that to the degree where I'm able to have a genuine, honest, great relationship with my father, and understand the amazing heroics, and see the goodness in the degree of egocentricity someone like my father has had to have to partake in the human journey, as opposed to resenting it, which was just coming from my retaliation of not knowing why it is that this behaviour was present, and why I was subjected to it. And I'm just able to leave that whole mess behind! And it does wonders for any part of a relationship and that's just an example of it.

[159] And I've been fortunate enough that my dad actually has now been able to understand the human condition as well, which has just paved a gateway for a whole different kind of relationship that I never actually expected I'd experience in my life-time, and I imagine that a lot of young men don't expect to experience with their father on a certain genuine level, where it's okay to reintroduce sensitivity and honesty, and all the old egocentric hierarchies can just go, and you can just talk to your father on an equal footing, honestly about the world, and you can just see the fundamental goodness in each other, and genuinely start to sympathise with each other's situation, which just makes the relationship unlike anything you experienced prior to understanding the human condition.

[160] **Alex Akritidis**: This information has completely changed my life, my relationship with family, my uncle and my little cousins. The way I approach my life is in such a different way, especially with my siblings. To be able to compassionately understand them and just be happy when they walk through the door, unlike when I was younger—because we have very different strategies so it was very easy to have a conflict there without understanding. So it's beautiful, absolutely beautiful.

[161] This has just *changed my life*. I remember the moment the information sunk in enough that I just saw that this is THE solution to the world's problems. I was on cloud nine. It brought me and my brother together, because me and my brother had opposite strategies [for managing life]—opposite strategies—and there was just no way in the resigned world without understanding that we were ever going to get along. And the same with my other siblings, and my family—before the information, my family was so dysfunctional and we would go out parading as if our family was more functional than others, and then now it's like I can see how dysfunctional it was and it's so relieving to now lift that burden of guilt. And obviously the rest of my family has this understanding, so we can all just come together. I always have visions of everybody just

being at one—adults and kids, no hierarchy; they're all just playing together and there's just unconditional nurturing and everyone is—not from a non-understanding point of view, not controlled by instincts—finally genuinely behaving cooperatively and lovingly, through understanding, and it's just crazy and it's just going to solve all the world's problems. I can see every problem right now is run by the human condition and once this understanding gets out there, everybody's just going to come together.

[162]**Katerina Akritidis**: I wanted to say before when you said how you and your son can talk as equals, that's how we are in our family—because now we can understand each other, in mostly all our conversations there's no hierarchy involved; we can just talk on equal terms, it's good.

[163]**Desi**: Without meaning to, the conversations just start on a daily basis; they're just constantly bouncing off ideas.

[164]**Katerina**: A year ago when mum and dad weren't so involved, the conversations at the dinner table were just old world, resigned stuff but now the human condition comes up all the time. We talk about it all the time.

[165]**Nicoletta Akritidis**: Even if we're not talking about the WTM, it's just always honesty and like you're always talking about things from a base of understanding and honesty and truth, so it's always good conversations, *good* conversations.

[166]**Desi**: Two years ago I would be saying whenever the kids amongst each other would be talking and I'd walk in I'd say, "Oh my God, *again*, you're talking about the human condition! How much can you talk about the human condition?!" And it's funny now because we've come so far...well, we've got a long way to go, I've got a long way to go...but yeah, now the conversations are happening and I don't see a problem, I'm actually liking the conversations!

[167] **Nicoletta**: It has changed my life completely. I have gotten a much better relationship with my siblings, from fighting most days, to now when I can finally understand everyone. Like my brothers, we've all got different strategies: one is quite 'power-addicted' and egocentric. That's kind of similar to my dad as well, and all the men in my family—always kind of being oppressive and telling me what to do—but then through the information I've been able to understand where that's coming from, and I can understand the role that men have played in the whole journey of understanding the human condition. And also with my dad—I mean, everyone really, all adults—I love when Jeremy says how you can understand why people have so much frustration, like volcanic amounts of anger, because we're suffering, and we've been suffering, from the human condition, for two million years, but I've definitely seen recently a big transformation within him.

[168] The family is meant to be something that represents togetherness and love, but that's not really common now, or ever, because we haven't ever understood the human condition. I think this understanding has really helped bring my family together, especially between the men and women in my family. When you can't stand each other, you're always conflicting, always fighting; my parents were always fighting, at one stage really badly, and now they don't fight as much, and nowhere near to the extent that they used to, because they can understand each other. We are genuinely a much more together, happy, secure family, not all the time of course, but you don't need to fake that anymore to the world because it's actually true. A lot of the time we are happy and actually loving and living with each other so genuinely and excitedly. We can actually spend hours on end all together. Just being able to enjoy each other's company is so special where families can't nowadays; people don't understand each other, everyone feels condemned by everyone around them, and you just can't talk deeply and honestly, and I think that's so special that we have that connection and I just want to make every

person in the world be able to have the connection that I have with my family. One day every family...I mean the whole world will be one big family...but immediate families can spend time with each other, can actually truly love each other and feel connected. That's a really nice vision to have.

———————————

[169] **Jeremy**: So that's a family who have been benefiting enormously from being able to understand the human condition!

[170] So don't forget that on our Transformation page, at www.humancondition.com/transformation, there are further wonderful examples like the Akritidis family of how being able to understand the human condition is able to therapise our lives—and also further inspiring examples of, and helpful instructions about, the Transformed Way of Living.

[171] Also, the transcript of my, Tony's, and this Akritidis video, are all presented in [this] *The Great Transformation* booklet, which is freely available on our website, or you can purchase it from book shops like Amazon.

[172] **And remember that the best way to help transform the world and yourself is to become involved in the World Transformation Movement**—visit our Community page at www.humancondition.com/community.

[173] Also, for guidance on how you can help promote these human-race-saving understandings, visit our 'How to Help' page at www.humancondition.com/how-to-help.

[174] A special thanks to WTM founding member James Press for his brilliant work filming and editing all our WTM studio presentations.

[175] And thank YOU very, very much for watching/reading this presentation.

Printed in the USA
CPSIA information can be obtained
at www.ICGtesting.com
LVHW060744301023
762473LV00036B/1153